MASTERING FEAR

MASTERING FEAR

The Ultimate Challenge

A Journey Facing the Emotion of Fear

By Steven Bisyak* & Michael McDermott

*Guinness Book of World Records Holder

PHOTOS: Courtesy of *Headshots*

Published in North America by

Latté Publishing
P.O. Box 3073
Kirkland, WA 98083-3073
(206) 821-9050

First Printing, May 1994

Printed in the USA   ISBN 0-9640871-1-1

Mastering Fear
The Ultimate Challenge

CONTENTS

INTRODUCTION

This book is intended to motivate the reader to recognize and then master his or her fears. The stories you're about to read are true. Personal power is only achieved by knowing what you want and being willing to risk action. Without action, nothing is achieved. Without risk, action is not possible. A person limited by fear is under the chains of false emotion. Any person who recognizes that *FEAR* is *False Evidence Appearing Real* and then takes action in spite of the fear has mastery over the fear.

As we considered material for inclusion in this book, we realized it contained interesting stories from Steven's personal experience that illustrate many of the points we're making. Therefore, wherever the pronoun "I" is used in the manuscript, with the exception of the Foreword by Michael, it refers to stories or illustrations from Steven's personal point of view.

ONLY A PERSON WHO RISKS IS FREE!

THE ACTIVITIES DESCRIBED IN THIS BOOK ARE DANGEROUS. THE AUTHORS AND PUBLISHERS OF THIS BOOK DISCLAIM ANY AND ALL LIABILITY FOR ACCIDENTS AND/OR INJURIES CAUSED BY PARTICIPATION IN THE ACTIVITIES DESCRIBED IN THIS BOOK AND WILL NOT BE HELD LIABLE IN THE EVENT OF SUCH ACCIDENTS OR INJURIES.

Michael McDermott

FOREWORD

I rolled into the parking lot of the Puyallup fairgrounds late in the afternoon. The sun was sinking low in the west and my heart was sinking as well. This was to be my first firewalk. A television crew was present. Oh, no, I wasn't walking. But I was there to observe and that was scary enough for me. I had come to watch firewalking. Fire and walk was a contradiction in my mind—walking on fire? No way!! I couldn't compute that.

I remembered playing with matches when I was a child. I built a small fire with a neighbor girl. We were very proud of ourselves for building that cute little fire all by ourselves. The fire was so very small and harmless, we both left and went home. Soon, I heard a great commotion. I ran out to the front porch of our house. My beloved woods were on fire! Without realizing it, I had started the woods next to our house on fire. Fortunately, a neighbor saw the blaze and called the fire department. Our house was barely saved from being destroyed by that fire.

Once a neighbor boy decided to walk through a pile of rubbish his parents burned in their yard. His clothing caught on fire and he was in the hospital for two months. I thought about that before I walked onto the Puyallup fairgrounds. Then I thought about something else.

Once my cousin's nightgown caught on fire and she was terribly burned. Walking on fire? That's crazy! I just couldn't conceive of it at all!

To me, fire was something you didn't touch. To my way of thinking, firewalking was impossible. Yet, here were people claiming that they could do it.

In spite of those dilemmas boiling through my mind, I strolled casually onto the fairgrounds. I tried my best to look cool, calm, confident—unafraid and unaffected. I was invited to the firewalk by Jim Jarvis, a firewalker whom I had met at the Lake Street Bakery and Social Club over two years previously. He had talked to me about firewalking for over two years, but his stories just went in one ear and out the other. When Jim started talking, I quit listening. None of it registered. I thought all that stuff about firewalking was just a big story he made up, and I felt sorry that he had to make up stories just to get attention. Especially when he talked about being a holder of a *Guinness Book* world record for the firewalk. I doubted if there was even such a category in the *Guinness Book*. I didn't even bother to look.

Jim said he was one of a group of people who walked barefoot on the hottest fire in the recorded history of the world. He said that he had been taught to firewalk by Steven Bisyak. He explained that Steven's group, Challenges Unlimited, Inc., had set that record and just one month later, they built a 120-foot long fire. They walked on that fire, and set a second new world's record for the longest firewalk in the world.

I arrived early at the Puyallup fairgrounds for the *Town Meeting* TV show, so I was able to get a pretty good seat in the lower bleachers. There were about 350 people from all walks of life. A group of people in front of me clutched Bibles in their hands. They huddled together in groups, bowing their heads and praying that Satan would be rebuked and that rain would pour down to put the fire out.

x

It was a beautiful, sunny day and there was no rain in the forecast for another month. They were praying that the firewalkers would get burned!

Their attitude astonished me. I considered myself to be a Christian. Praying for people to get hurt and burned seemed to me to be the opposite of what Christ taught. I thought the firewalkers were doing something really dangerous, taking their lives in their hands to try to help people understand something pretty awesome. I admired their courage. I was concerned for Jim and the rest of the walkers, fearing that some of them might get burned.

Ken Schram, host of the *Town Meeting* program, started interviewing Steven Bisyak. He was definitely playing the "devil's advocate," trying to put Steven on the defensive, for the sake of controversy. There was a skeptic seated next to Steven. The skeptic interrupted, contradicting and refuting nearly everything Steven said. The skeptic said he had a Band-Aid taped to his foot. He would be willing to run across the fire to prove to the audience that the fire wasn't hot! This was in spite of the fact that the optical pyrometer in the fire recorded the temperature at 1122°. The skeptic said that the fire wouldn't conduct enough heat to his foot to burn the Band-Aid. After he galloped across the fire, the skeptic tore the Band-Aid off his foot and gave it to Ken Schram. The Band-Aid was singed. Several firewalkers from the audience were called on to give some very convincing on-camera testimonies about the positive benefits of firewalking.

The fire was huge! It was over 25 feet long. It was so hot, you couldn't stand within 12 feet of it! A steak was thrown on the coals, and it quickly fried to a crisp. After the steak cooled, the crisp was given to Mort, the *Town Meeting* mascot. The dog ate the crisp.

That night, after the firewalk, I attended an AA meeting. When it came my turn to talk at the meeting, I told everybody how I had overcome my fear and went to watch a real firewalk. After I spoke, somebody passed me a business card. The card said, *Challenges Unlimited, Inc., Steven Bisyak, President*. The couple that sent me that card said they wanted to speak to me after the meeting. We drove to Denny's Restaurant for something to eat. The man had been to a firewalk in North Bend. He told me some unbelievable stories. "Not only do they walk on fire," he said, "they swing through trees that are 75 to 100 feet high! These people also bend huge concrete reinforcing bars with their necks. Both men and women break bricks, boards, and even rocks with their bare hands!!" It was unbelievable. I didn't know what to think of this. I was curious. I wondered if any of it could possibly be true.

About a week after the *Town Meeting* show, I ran into Jim Jarvis and he conned me into giving him a ride to a firewalk. I was pretty scared, but I think he knew I would walk on that fire. He introduced me to Steven Bisyak. Steven and I sat down on the tailgate of his 3/4-ton Chevy pickup truck. It said *FIREWLK* on the license plate. The windows were plastered with stickers that said, *I Walk On Fire, I Can Do Anything I Choose*" and "*Firewalkers Kick Ash!* Metallic signs on the doors said, *Challenges Unlimited, Inc.—Firewalking—Guinness Book of World Records Holder*. At that time, Steven regularly sponsored two or more firewalks a month at his five-acre property in North Bend. That's a lot of hard work. It requires a great deal of focus and dedication. It takes a lot of work cutting, hauling, and splitting very heavy wood. There's also an enormous liability assumed by any person who teaches the firewalk. There are real dangers associated with firewalking.

My experience has taught me that firewalking isn't very dangerous as long as people follow the instructions and pay attention. Unfortunately, people don't always pay attention and they don't always follow instructions. That's when people can get hurt, even seriously. I've been hurt because I wasn't paying attention.

Steven talked about the importance of intention, the nature of fear, and the importance of taking action. The motto of Challenges Unlimited, Inc., is: *5% Talk, 95% Action.* Steven told me that firewalking is a metaphor that stands for the challenges life offers us. He said that if I learned the principles of firewalking, I could use those principles to overcome fear and obstacles that limited me in my life, and that nothing would be impossible for me to accomplish in this life.

It was a beautiful evening. The sun went down and the stars came out over Steven's property in North Bend. We were surrounded by mountains, the sky was clear, and the full moon rose through the trees. It smelled fresh and clean out there in the open woods. We were completely surrounded by trees, except for one large plush patch of green lawn there in the forest. The firepit sat in the middle of the bright emerald green, freshly mowed lawn.

There was a very colorful and odd assortment of characters at my first firewalk. I wanted to meet them all, to learn their secrets of walking on fire. What makes a firewalker tick? I was very curious to find that out. I was especially impressed with Jeff. He helped me a lot, not only at my first firewalk, but at later firewalks when I actually forgot how to walk on fire. Jeff patiently explained it all to me again.

Steven taught me how to firewalk that night. I'm going to skip the details of that, because the rest of this book is literally chock full and crammed with keys and clues about how to do that. When the fire was finally raked out, there was a lot of radiant heat coming from it. I couldn't stand very close to the fire because of the intense heat. I did manage to walk on the hot coals that night, about six times. Another guy who rode up to the firewalk with us walked on the fire before I did. Then he walked over to the brick stand and busted a brick with his hand. I wouldn't allow myself to swing my fist down with full force on a brick, because I was working in a corporate law firm as a word processor at the time. I was afraid that if I swung my hand down on that brick, my hand would break, and I'd be out of a job.

After walking on the fire, I was completely inspired, completely uplifted and encouraged. It was an emotional high! It was a great thrill, totally inspiring! I made a commitment to myself to firewalk for at least a year. I felt very lucky, very fortunate indeed. I was grateful to be among a small group of individuals who had set the Guinness Book of World Records for firewalking in 1987. Both of those records stand to this very day. What an unusual thing to do! I didn't know many people who had done anything nearly that cool. I wanted to get to know all the members of Challenges Unlimited, Inc. I also wanted to get to know myself better, and I figured firewalking was the best way for me to do that. I would become a firewalker!

Soon, I started volunteering to help out with Challenges Unlimited, Inc. I typeset the monthly newsletter for awhile. I said that I wanted to write a book with Steven. I would interview him, do all the writing, Steven would promote the book on TV and radio, and we would work as a team, sharing 50-50 in the enterprise.

I mentioned my background as an English major and the fact that I had already been a professional writer for the McGraw-Hill Company. I was also a published poet and had been a songwriter for many years.

Steven was immediately interested. For years, he dreamed of writing a book. We agreed at that time to start work. We made the decision to self-publish, at least for the first year or so. I initiated the project by interviewing Steven. My initial interview resulted in the first chapter of this book. I brought the finished chapter to Steven and he really liked it. Early one winter morning, I jumped in my white 1968 vintage Mercedes and drove to North Bend. We stopped for a latté and headed back to the office. Steven stood for several hours, pacing around his office, surrounded by books, crystals, and newspaper articles, while I sat down at the computer. We cooked up a chapter right then and there. We kicked ideas around and wrote them down as they seemed to materialize right out of thin air.

In my experience, it's a scary thing to publish your first book. It's a step into the unknown if you've never done it before. It's the first time. It means stepping out into the community and making a major statement. You might get criticized, or even condemned. You might fail or, on the other hand, you might succeed beyond your wildest dreams! You could even become a movie star if you're not careful. Life as you've always known it might turn to dust. You would be more visible, and perhaps have less privacy, especially if a picture of your mug is out there on the cover of some book. I've already been accused of egotism. Okay, you guys, you win, I guess I'm in love with myself, what can I say? Because you can't be invisible any more, it's hard to remain anonymous. These are concerns and fears that come along with writing books.

Steven and I, as any first-time published author will attest, had to work through some major fears involved with becoming published authors. That process is no different from firewalking; in fact, it is a major "firewalk." But, what an interesting and exciting firewalk it is!

Over a period of days, weeks, and years, I got to know Steven. We became friends. I recognized immediately that he is a great storyteller. From his days in Alaska as a mountain man, his experiences with mountain climbing and crystal mining, and his adventures leading the firewalk over the years, as well as setting the *Guinness Book* world record for firewalking, made him a very colorful character indeed.

Becoming a member of Challenges Unlimited, Inc., was the start of a big adventure for me. As a member of Challenges Unlimited, I have been challenged to walk on fire, do cartwheels in the fire, somersault in the fire, stand in the fire, bungee jump, hang-glide, rappel, have my head shaved, become a certified instructor of firewalking, body pierce, break bricks, boards, and rocks with my bare hands, and bend steel reinforcing bars with my throat. Every physical challenge you could imagine was available to us as a group. It was great!

What are the limits to the power of the mind? Are there any limits to the incredible human potential? We were beginning to feel that there were basically no limits to how much we could learn from each other and from our frequent and magical experiences with firewalking.

One time Steven invited me to pick up and handle one of his pet python snakes. He had two pythons. This one was about three feet long. I had a lifelong fear of snakes. Steven enjoys helping people face and overcome their fears, no matter what those fears are. Many times, I've seen him so inspired by another person's courage that tears welled up in his eyes. You don't see too many men doing that these days.

A couple of weeks ago, out of the blue, I got a call from Steven. He was in Seattle. He wanted to get together. When we got together, we agreed it was time to finish our book. Steven wanted to complete the project in one week (unheard of!), so that he could surprise his mother by giving her the first copy hot off the press for her 60th birthday. The book was finished in just one week, in plenty of time for Steven's mother's 60th birthday!

It's very gratifying for me personally to see our book, *Mastering Fear: The Ultimate Challenge* rolling "hot" off the presses. This has been a dream of mine for a long time now. That dream has become a reality! When I started work on this book, I figured it would be polished off and hot off the press in about three months. It just didn't happen that way. The job of writing a book is enormous, let alone printing and publishing a book. Writing the book from Steven's point of view has been an extra challenge for me, and I'm proud of this accomplishment.

I had a mixture of reasons for writing this book. First of all, I wanted to get to know Steven better. I wanted to learn everything he had to teach, to con and coax it all out of him. I thought Steven was a particularly colorful and interesting character. His stories amused and entertained me. I wanted not just to be a good firewalker—my ambition was to be a great firewalker. I figured if anybody on the planet could show me how to firewalk, it was Steven. I wanted to learn everything I could about the power of the mind, the ability to focus, and what it takes to become an unlimited human being. This was not just another good story, another entertaining book. This was a blockbuster book, a message so powerful, it simply had to get out!

It's been an inspiration and a joy for me to put this information into its current form. Every time I help someone with what I've received as a result of firewalking, I feel great!

It is appropriate for me to introduce Steven Bisyak, a man I've written about for over three years now. Anybody who reads this book will be blessed and benefitted by it. I know that for sure, because I certainly have been. This knowledge is like money in the bank. If it is applied, it can help you again and again and again. The more this knowledge is used, the more powerful it grows. Nothing turns me on more than seeing people achieve their dreams. This is the stuff of which life is made. Going for dreams. Accomplishing in spite of impossible odds. It's pure inspiration, and inspiration is life. Whether it's walking across a fire, making money, starting a relationship, starting a business, cleaning up the environment, or spiritual enlightenment, it's my belief that we can accomplish it if we just have the know-how. Anyone who diligently applies the principles outlined in this book will find that they're able to go way beyond their own fear and self-limitation. I believe we're all here on this planet together to help one another achieve our dreams and not to be defeated by fear or limited by failure and negativity. Knowledge is power. This book is knowledge, and this book is power. *Use this power wisely*. This book is also entertainment, a collection of great stories that are a lot of fun to read. I counsel you to buy this book and to read it as soon as possible. The benefits you gain will be immediate in your life. It will grow on you, I guarantee it. Read it again and again and again. You will benefit more each time.

I wish you all the very best that life has to offer. See you at a firewalk!

Michael McDermott is co-author of *Mastering Fear: The Ultimate Challenge* with Steven Bisyak; and author of *Stories of the Fire*. He is an International Seminar Leader and Sundoor Certified Firewalking Instructor.

Dedicated to

Our Parents

and

All People Who Overcome Fear

Steven Bisyak
A Journey Facing the Emotion of Fear

1

FROM INTROVERT TO
THRILL-SEEKER: STEVEN'S STORY

Come on Baby, Light My Fire

I had my first exposure to the firewalk when I was about nine years old. I saw it on a TV program titled *You Asked For It*. I was amazed to see people walking on red-hot coals without getting burned. What mysterious power was it that gave people this seeming immunity against fire? These people appeared super-human to me. My parents had made me well aware that if I came in contact with fire, I would get burned. Strangely, I was watching people walking on hot coals safely without burning themselves. I was mystified. I couldn't figure it out. How did they do that?

Then in early 1984, a friend invited me to go to a firewalk. "A what?" I asked.

He said, "A firewalk! You know, it's where you go walking bare-footed on hot coals." My memory of the TV show *You Asked For It* popped into my mind immediately.

I remembered seeing people walk on blazing hot red coals. I responded, "Yes, let's go do it. Firewalking has always fascinated me. I'd really like to be there." I wanted to witness firsthand how people could do such a fantastic thing. I had no intention of doing it myself, however. I just wanted to observe and understand. Did people go into trances or altered states of mind? How could people walk on fire without getting burned?

The workshop was facilitated by Tolly Burkan. Tolly has been teaching firewalking since about 1978. Tolly talked about the nature of fear and illusion. "What we think is reality," he said, "and what appears to be factual is not necessarily true. You can change your mental programming instantaneously if you know how to do it. You don't have to spend years in psychotherapy trying to figure out where all your erroneous programming came from. You can simply change your programming." This was big news to me. It was the beginning of a great turnaround in the way I perceived the world.

After Tolly's talk, the fire burned down to the point it was ready to rake into a 20-foot-long coal bed. We all strolled out to the fire with our shoes off. I watched Tolly carefully massage the coal bed with his rake. Then he squirted the rake with a hose. It made a tremendous "Pshhhhhsssssshhhhhtttttt" sound as a cloud of white-hot steam shot high up into the night sky. "Holy Moses, that coal bed is hot as a forge!" I muttered to myself. We cautiously approached the 20-foot-long pathway of hot coals. It was so sweltering that I had to stand back to avoid getting my face blistered.

Peggy walked first. I stood watching Peggy Dylan. She was wearing a beautiful white dress. She seem to float across the coals. I admired her grace as she slowly strolled over the coals. Peggy Dylan is the female originator of the contemporary firewalking movement. She's a renowned firewalk instructor and international seminar leader. She's also the founder of the Sundoor Foundation for Transpersonal Education. Then I observed Tolly carefully as he walked through the coals. I discounted his walk. I figured he knew something the rest of us didn't know. I thought there must be a magic trick. If I watched closely enough, maybe I could learn the trick.

I was surprised to see two boys, seven and eight years old, prancing through the gnarly crimson coal bed. After seeing those kids walk, I was startled into an awareness that *my body was moving toward the coal bed*. A voice somewhere inside my mind began screaming, "What are you doing! You don't have any insurance!! You're supposed to go to work tomorrow!! You're going to end up in the Harborview burn ward, you idiot!!" My mind raced. "What if I burn? What if I can't work? What will my mom say? What if I end up in a wheelchair?"

I marched toward the front edge of that coal bed. I hit what I would call a *wall of fear*. It seemed like it was four feet thick. It seemed to me that the fear materialized; it seemed as real as a concrete wall. This wall of fear stopped me from taking another step. My feet froze in place. I couldn't move. I stood there shaking, my knees knocking together. It suddenly dawned on me that fear was an emotional reaction I had felt every single day of my life. Fear was really nothing new or unfamiliar to me.

I had never experienced fear as powerfully and as intensely as I did that night. I felt the fiery blast of heat from the coal bed. The air seemed to shimmer in hot blasts. All at once my fear turned to anger. "BULL!!!" I thought. *"Fear is not going to limit me!!!"* I lurched forward quickly, stepping into the red-hot coal bed. A shock of amazement shot through my body. As my feet buried themselves in red-hot coals, I realized there was no perceptible heat on my feet. It was uncanny. I stepped to the far end of the coal bed where I stopped and examined my feet. I stood there, overwhelmed and mystified. I counted my toes one by one to make sure they were still all there: one, two, three, four, five, six, seven, eight, nine, ten—sure enough, they were all there! None had melted, none had fried. "Did I really do what I think I did? Did I really walk on that coal bed? Was it an hallucination?" I asked myself. I had to do it again, in spite of Tolly's instructions to walk only once. I had just walked over a 1200° coal bed. I didn't experience any heat on the soles of my feet. There was no pain. "I've got to experience this again to make sure I really did what I thought I just did," I said. I passed through the fire a second time.

The second time through, I walked very slowly, bending over at the waist. I watched the coals as closely as possible. Again, I felt no heat on my feet. I was walking so slowly that it seemed I was almost standing in the fire. I was incredulous. It just blew me away. I couldn't figure out how this thing worked.

The night after my first firewalk, my mind raced with visions of the experience. I couldn't sleep. One by one, I took a mental inventory of my belief system.

I realized the firewalk had just blown a big hole in my belief system. How could I be sure anything I believed was true? I walked on fire without being burned! I knew that was impossible. How could this be?

When I awoke the next morning, I ran to the window, scanning the horizon for smoke. I had to find another fire. I needed to firewalk again. It was the single most positive, mind-blowing, empowering experience I had ever had. I had never confronted my own fear more solidly and vigorously. Many changes were soon to take place in my life.

Three weeks after my first firewalk, I invited a lady to go on a first date. I called it a "hot date," since I was taking her to a firewalk.

Tolly Burkan had left town the day after my first firewalk, so there was a different instructor at my second firewalk. The fire was tiny, less than six feet long. The puny fire was raked out into a two and one-half-foot-wide coal bed. It looked ridiculously small. I was actually amused. I knew I was a master firewalker. This fire would hold no challenge for a guy like me. Firewalker extraordinaire. "What a teeny-weenie little two-bit fire! This'll be a piece of cake." I was somewhat humiliated. My date wouldn't get to see me in all my glory walking on a great big long fire. "No problem," I told her, "I've done this before."

The instructor walked the fire first. I was chomping at the bit. I really wanted to show off, and secretly wished I could have been the first one across. I wasn't feeling any fear. In that moment I was cocky, absolutely sure of myself. The wall of fear I confronted at my first firewalk was not there at all. My ego swelled.

5

Proudly, I glanced at my date to make sure her eyes were on me. After I made sure of this, I said, "Hey! Look at me walk on this fire!" My feet hit the fire. I started trucking over that little coal bed.

Time stopped.

In a flash it became one of the longest fires I have ever walked on. The heat was so intense I felt the bottom of my feet melting off, the instant they hit the coals. With each step the process of cooking my flesh continued. It happened so fast, even Jumpin' Jack Flash couldn't have escaped. The damage was done, faster than the speed of thought. As fast as the speed of light. My feet were so badly burned, I had to crawl to the bathroom for the next two weeks. My ego took a severe beating that night.

During my weeks of healing, I reflected on that disastrous burn. I asked myself a lot of questions. Why does fire burn a person one time, and not another? Why does fire sometimes burn only one foot and not the other? Why only specific places on the foot? Why not the whole foot? I dreaded the prospect of getting another excruciating burn. Yet, I knew I had to go back. Curiosity killed the cat. If I had to be a burned cat, so be it. My fear was bigger than ever, bigger than it was even in my first firewalk. I had to get some answers. I had to firewalk again. I was obsessed and consumed by the prospect. I had to go back for my third firewalk.

If you fall off the horse
Get back on the horse

I've learned by my life experience that whenever I confront my fear, I need to step out and take a risk. Whenever I risk, an accident or an injury can occur, but accidents can and do happen, even when I'm not taking a risk! So, what the hell have I got to lose? I become bigger than the fear, and the fear doesn't limit me any more! I've learned that accidents and injuries are nothing more than learning experiences. I do my best to avoid them, but if they do happen, I haven't really lost much. A minor accident might even prevent something more serious from happening in the future.

If you get a little blister from firewalking . . . Walk again and cauterize that blister!!

A friend once said, "Always expect the unexpected." His other classic gem was, "Always expect the expected." Life can be full of interest and excitement, but there is always some risk involved. I'm learning to accept the world the way it is, not the way I'd like it to be. I knew what it felt like to walk on fire and feel no heat on my feet. I walked uninjured my first time, without blisters or burns. That was the most incredible feeling of empowerment I had in my entire life. My second firewalk showed me what it was like to walk across the coal bed full of ego and literally cook my feet.

The night of my third firewalk, I stood in front of the fire, hesitating. Fear wouldn't allow me to move. My eyes watered. All I could think about was the memory of burning my feet on my second firewalk.

My fear of pain was overwhelming in that moment. The voices started to sound off inside my head. "You're chicken. You can't do it, you'll burn again." Another voice said, "If you don't walk again, you'll be afraid the rest of your life." I felt helpless.

A friend named Vic walked up to me. Tears welled in my eyes. Vic put his arm around me and said, "Steven, whenever you want to do something in your life, *just blank your mind and go*."

Immediately my mind seemed to go blank. Thoughts vanished; visions of burning myself disappeared. I forgot my doubt, my fear, and my pain. In my next conscious moment I was strolling on my third fire and there was *absolutely no heat in that fire!!* I knew I could do it. I would go across the fire again and again and again!!

"I did it! I did it! I did it!!!" I kept congratulating myself. I was higher than a kite. I knew in that instant that no matter what the pain, no matter what the odds, nothing, not even fire, could stop me from going forward in my life in spite of my fear. I cried more when I got across that third fire than I did standing in front of it, paralyzed by fear. My tears were tears of joy and ecstasy.

My ordeal at my third firewalk was the challenge that opened my mind to the possibilities of mastering fear in all areas of my life. I became determined that fear would no longer limit me from moving to accomplish my dreams.

Whatever you want to be . . .
Assume the role and you'll be it!

Steven Bisyak

My fear went back a long way. One of my biggest fears has always been the fear of public speaking. When I was in high school, I took an "F" on an oral book report. When the teacher called on me, my knees knocked and my throat tightened so badly I couldn't get out of my chair. I was too afraid to speak in front of 30 of my classmates, in spite of the fact that I had been in school with those kids for six years. Most of them, in fact, were very close friends. It was easier to face the wrath of my father and take an "F" on my report than it was to give that speech.

Within one month after walking on fire, my income in my contracting business doubled. I call that "taking the firewalk to the bank." I took on jobs I previously believed were beyond my ability. I was still afraid, but that didn't stop me. The firewalk gave me the confidence to do things that I thought were impossible for me to achieve. I just used the same techniques to walk through my fears that I had used to walk on fire. Using the energy of fear meant I was able to take action. That translated into money when I applied it to my business. I had not learned to firewalk in order to make more money, but that was what was happening. I was soon making money hand over fist, more money than I'd ever made in my life.

For the first time in my life, I was able to crack through denial and take a penetrating look at all my fears. I admitted the fears that had been limiting me from doing the things I wanted to do. I attended every firewalking workshop I could find. I spent thousands of dollars, but it was worth every penny. I was convinced that the firewalk was so valuable, I would have gladly spent over a million dollars on it. It was like putting together a jigsaw puzzle of the entire universe.

My life started changing dramatically. The guy I thought I was started to vanish, and a new person of greater courage and ability came forward.

This process was the greatest thrill of my life. I understood that I could step through my fear and accomplish my wildest dreams.

I had habitually allowed fear to limit my life. These same fears had been so powerful they almost stopped me from walking on fire. I had a whole kit-bag of them. Economic insecurity. Low self-esteem. Fear of criticism. Fear of people. Fear of rejection. Fear that I wasn't worthy. Fear of injury. Fear that my life would change. I noticed that when insecurity and fear got the best of me, I would get into self-pity and depression. Both drained me and I couldn't take action.

In the beginning, firewalking was very scary to me. Whenever I faced a fire, it was as if I were facing that fire for the very first time in my life. My attitude about it changed. The firewalk gave me the tools to look at my fears and to walk through those fears. I would look at the worst that could possibly happen, and then accept it. Then I'd let my horror thoughts go. I focused on the best and took action. The results were amazing!

I realized fear was there to sharpen my senses and remind me to pay attention. I learned to allow fear to pass through me rather than letting it freeze me into inaction. I was so excited about firewalking that I wanted to teach others how to firewalk and master all their fears. I realized that firewalking is an extremely powerful tool. It certainly helped me realize more of my potential. My desire was to teach others how to step through their fears and not be limited by fear.

If I could do that, I felt my life would have meaning. I would be doing something tremendously positive that would make a difference in the world.

I always thought of myself as just one of the crowd, just another very average person. Nothing special. But I was an average person who discovered a mighty powerful tool to help people change their lives. I am very grateful for this, and consider myself to be a very lucky person because of it!

One day I sat in a hot mineral bath at Harbin Hot Springs, California. A friend was asking me about firewalking. Suddenly he turned to me and asked me a question point-blank. "We've got about 70 people here who want to learn to firewalk. Will you teach us how to do it?"

I reacted with great fear at the prospect of actually teaching other people how to firewalk. What if they didn't follow directions and got burned? Would I feel guilty? Would I be able to live with myself? In spite of the fear and short notice, I rose to the challenge. "Yes! Count me in! I'll do it." Two days was short notice indeed to prepare for something as awesome and scary as conducting my first firewalking workshop, but I did it.

The Fire is the Teacher

That humble beginning in 1984 sparked my career of teaching other people how to firewalk and how to accomplish their dreams. Since that spontaneous beginning, I've led over 10,000 people through the fire. I've walked on fire myself over 1400 times.

11

Fear of fire has been transformed into a much more manageable feeling for me now. However, I still experience fear in my life, and walking on fire is still a challenge. I have a healthy respect for the power of fire. The number of times I've successfully walked on fire means nothing if my mental state isn't right. The fire doesn't know if you've walked on it once or a thousand times. It makes no difference. You can still get burned.

It's like flying an airplane. A pilot can successfully fly over a mountain range a thousand times, but if the altitude and the attitude of the plane are too low on flight 1001, it's going to crash. If a person's attitude is not right, you can "crash" in the fire. The fire is no respecter of persons. It doesn't know if you're worth $10 billion or if you're flat busted. You can get blistered or burned, and you can't buy your way out of the trial by fire. You've got to have guts to do it. That applies to women as well as men, and I've known some mighty awesome woman firewalkers.

> *It's your attitude not your altitude*
> *that determines how high*
> *you'll go in life*
>
> ## Zig Ziglar

Attitude can also determine whether or not a person gets blistered in the firewalk. For the spiritually inclined, the experience of firewalking puts people in touch with a higher power. Because fire is one of the elements, firewalking puts one in touch with nature.

Your bare feet are grounded solidly on mother earth. You come in contact with the fire. You're out under the open sky in the fresh air. It's great to sit around the "campfire" and talk or sing before the fire burns down to coals. Then the coals are raked out into a hot coal bed. We've had rock 'n roll firewalks with loud music. We've also had firewalks that are so quiet you could hear a pin drop. Most of the time, after we cross the fire, we lighten up a lot. We start expressing a playful mood. We keep doing it, because it's a lot of fun. In reality, people very seldom get blisters. After some of our firewalks, we even roast corn, delicious baked over hot coals.

The firewalk reminds me that fear is such a familiar feeling. The firewalk allows me to use fear as an ally. The real firewalks are the challenges that life hands us on a daily basis. Sometimes the "firewalk of life" is something as simple as getting across a crosswalk without getting killed by a car. Better pay attention! Most accidents occur when people are distracted. The firewalk is really a dress rehearsal for stepping through the fears and challenges life hands us. I'm not at war with my fear any more. I just accept and honor my fear. It has a place in my life. The firewalk taught me to make plans and really follow through with them.

I've made a commitment to do positive things. If I sense that I'm afraid to do them, and they're worthwhile, that's all the more reason to take action and step through my fear. This has become a habit with me. When you accept your fear and face your fear, you discover that meeting challenges and difficulties becomes a positive habit. Fear dissolves. When I step through it, it's not there any more!

A lot of times, I bust out laughing. I laugh at the illusion. Fear is such an illusion, created by the mind. You actually use up the energy of the fear and it disappears when you take action. If you don't face fear, you're bound to live with it forever because you're not allowing yourself to feel it, accept it, and walk through it. If you focus on fear, it gets bigger and bigger. It's a big boogey man. It terrorizes you. It becomes overwhelming until it's like a huge brick wall—it's all you can see. It's much easier to "face the music" and face the fear than to deny it and be at war with yourself forever. Life can become limited and dreams can be crushed by fear. Letting fear rule one's life is like being a prisoner of one's own thoughts.

I don't want to be limited by false beliefs about fear. I once believed that if I walked on fire I would get burned. To walk on fire and not get burned still impresses the hell out of me. It causes me constantly to challenge all my other beliefs about life and to look for the source of all my fears. My personal goal is to recognize, admit, and master my own fears. This erases all my self-limiting beliefs. It allows me to live my life with the greatest possible amount of freedom.

I'm committed to continue recognizing and facing fear in my life. I want to do all I can to help others experience the success that comes with mastering fear. I intend to keep walking through fear, doing all the things I previously believed I couldn't do.

I am taking action and accomplishing my dreams and desires. I will use the powerful energies of fear, converting them to excitement, and accomplishing what I want in my life.

14

Fear is caused by ignorance. How can you pass judgment on something you know nothing about? Once you've experienced something, you can say, "Okay, I didn't like that," or "It was GREEEAAATTT!!!!! When can we do it again????" If you see someone having a ball doing something you don't want to do, that's a sure sign you're probably afraid of doing it. Chances are you're in denial of your fear. Most of us are that way; we're all in the same boat. I've found by experience that fear of the unknown is the greatest fear most of us ever face.

Our creative nature follows the creative tendencies of the mind, which means that most of us think negative thoughts most of the time. The mind naturally creates negative thoughts and ideas. We can visualize disaster immediately. We have something like a movie theater of the mind that creates negative images, negative pictures, and negative outcomes. The firewalking workshop gives the tools to overcome these negative mental projections.

There have been a number of things I was afraid to do. For instance, I was petrified the first time I bungee jumped, but now I've bungee jumped 700 times. It's still scary, yet tremendously exciting. A couple of years ago, I went paragliding for the first time. It was a blast! I jumped off a 2500-foot mountain and caught a rising thermal of heated air. I flew my glider in the beautiful blue skies of Eastern Washington for over 45 minutes. I looked down on beautiful orchards and pastures along the banks of the mighty Columbia River.

Skydiving scared the hell out of me until I actually did it. Once I took that leap of faith out of the airplane, I was flying through the air, having an absolute blast!

I highly recommend skydiving to anyone who has any fear of heights. I've rappeled, and I've played with tarantulas and pythons, in spite of my initial fear and ignorance. I've done a number of body pierces with five-inch doll needles. I break bricks and rocks with my bare hands. Before I did those things, I believed it was actually impossible for me to do them. I was afraid the first time I ever did them, and I still feel fear whenever I do them. After you've done those things a number of times, though, the fear definitely diminishes. But it's still there.

> *Yesterday is a canceled check*
> *Tomorrow is a promissory note*
> *TODAY is cash in the hand*

I've faced physical challenges all my life, as well as emotional and mental fears. I've worked through financial insecurities and I've helped people deal with trouble on the job. There are a number of books and seminars on the market today that show people how to do those things. A mighty big challenge for most people is in the area of handling human relationships. Accepting fear and anger is important to healing wounds we inflict on others and ourselves. Physical challenges force us to face our fears. They have a direct and beneficial effect on our ability to handle all of life's problems.

Ultimately what the firewalk can do for you is to alter your perceptions of reality. When I was young, my parents warned me not to touch anything hot because it would burn me.

Belief is analogous to the roots of a tree, with the trunk and branches being the totality of one's mental programming. When you walk on fire and you don't get burned, you're contradicting the roots of your mental programming. In this way, erroneous beliefs start to crumble. You get free. Then you can change your beliefs if they no longer serve you. In other words, you can change the "tree" of your mental programming.

Many people live their lives mistakenly believing they're different from other people. They think they can't do a lot of the things that other people can do. The reality is that any functional person can do anything that any other functional person can do. The only difference between someone who accomplishes something and someone who doesn't is an attitude of mind. After my first firewalk, I examined all my beliefs one by one, asking the question, "Is this belief true, or is it false?"

I was really ticked off when I realized I had accepted quite a few false beliefs and ideas that limited me. I took a long, hard look at myself and asked, "What's real and what's illusion here?" That was the beginning of a continuing process I still go through. You never really complete the process, because more "stuff" comes up.

Every time I walk on a fire I learn more about myself. My mental state may change from one fire to the next and my emotions may be different at any given time, but before my foot comes in contact with hot burning coals, I have to check in. I have to ask myself the questions, How am I feeling right now? What's going on with me? How's my energy right now? What fears do I have right now? Have I set my ego aside?

When I walked on fire out of ego, I didn't respect the coal bed or the experience. I was more concerned with what other people were thinking of me. That can cause a blister.

> *The saddest words*
> *of tongue or pen*
> *are these four words:*
> *it might have been*

Rudyard Kipling

If you've never walked on fire before, I highly recommend that you just go do it. The reason for this is simple. When you're thinking about confronting your fear, many thoughts will play out in your mind. Thoughts like, "What if I burn, what if I trip and fall down in the fire, or what will my mother say?" Those thoughts are just examples of how restless the mind can get just before you're about to make a major breakthrough.

Most burns that occur at a firewalk are minor, consisting of small blisters or dry skin. The odds of a person getting seriously burned on his or her first firewalk are very small indeed.

All fear is based in ignorance. For example, hang gliding initially was something I was afraid to do because I was ignorant about it. I had no interest in hang gliding until I researched the subject. I discovered information that convinced me that hang gliding is safe for me.

18

If I discovered that one person out of every five who flies off a mountain with a hang glider crashed and died, I probably would not have done it at all. Every time I take action, I take a hard look at the risk versus the benefits. If it's too risky, I won't do it. The level of acceptable risk is something that varies from individual to individual. I learned that not one person died in ten years of hang gliding off this same 1500-foot mountain. The risk was very low indeed. As far as I was concerned, the benefits of confronting the fear involved in hang gliding were very high. There were about a dozen people in our group who went hang gliding. Everyone was completely ecstatic after the experience. We all agreed that hang gliding is awesome!

One time I lost a dear friend who was only 26 years old. He was the epitome of health, an excellent athlete with a superb sense of balance. His tragic, untimely death resulted from a simple fall in the bathtub. He fell and hit his nose on the edge of the toilet, driving the nasal bone into his brain. He died instantly. A few days later, his wife was on her way home from the funeral when her car ran off the road and hit a telephone pole, killing their eldest daughter. I'll never forget that as long as I live. That sad series of events opened my eyes. I realize that life is short, and time is fleeting. For every human being, time on this earth eventually runs out. I resolved that I would not be on my deathbed someday saying, "*I wish I had done this. I wish I had done that. If only I had taken action.*"

As you read these words, *make a decision now*. Take positive action and do something worthwhile you've been putting off.

There are no guarantees on tomorrow. Take action and do the things your heart tells you to do. There's just one thing you can be sure of. You do have this moment, *NOW*. That's really all there is in this experience of life. Yesterday is gone and tomorrow isn't here yet.

You can't really live in the past or in the future. When tomorrow gets here, it will become today; it will become now. The only time we ever really have is right now. You never know when your number might be up. If you're going to do anything, begin it now. It's literally now or never. Decide to take action in the moment, which is now. Making no decision is really making a decision. The decision is to procrastinate.

Procrastination is the Thief of Time

Procrastinating means putting things off. Putting things off robs people of opportunities that may never come their way again.

Hours become days, days become weeks, weeks become months, months become years. Before you know it, you've denied yourself for too long. It's too late. If you're lucky enough to live that long, you'll eventually get too old and too worn out to accomplish your dreams. So take action NOW. Get on the ball. Get rolling. Get into gear and accomplish all the things you want in life.

Extreme measures create extreme change. If you don't want your life to change, I don't recommend walking on fire. At age 19, I thought I had the world by the tail. I was a construction superintendent for a very wealthy corporation, the youngest person ever to hold that position. I really thought I had my life together.

On the other hand, even though my life was good and my ego told me I was the greatest, at times I could be an extremely negative person. Following that line of thought, I got caught up in the illusion that life sucks. The firewalk experience made me realize that I didn't have my head together at all. I had a good job, but I allowed my life to be limited by fear. After the firewalk, I realized my life is what I make it. It's good or it's bad, expanding or limiting, according to my thoughts. Now I know that I'm 100% responsible for what I make of my life. I create my own quality of life by the way I think and act in this world. If I decide to make it so, the world really can be a beautiful place.

TOMORROW NEVER COMES

*The time to take action is now . . .
because no matter what time it is
it's always now*

Michael McDermott

After learning to firewalk, I stepped into a new awareness of reality. My perceptions changed. Things became beautiful. I know they always have been and always will be beautiful. But I was awakened to the truth. This world really is what I make it. It can be a bowl of cherries or it can be the pits. My perceptions of reality are born out of what I choose to focus my attention on.

21

I create my own reality by what I choose to focus on, what I pay attention to.

To live life fully demands action. If I hadn't taken action, there is no way I could have set the *Guinness Book of World Records* for the hottest firewalk in recorded history. I did that. But it took a lot of action. It took a lot of wood, for one thing—two cords' worth. When you stand in front of a coal bed, you won't get across by wishful thinking. You have to take action and walk. Wishing things will happen won't cause them to happen. You have to work and take action.

2

I EXPERIENCE A FALL

My dad and I built a three-story tree house. When I was about 15 years old, the weekly TV show *Wild Wild West* was very popular. All the neighborhood kids were fascinated by a zipline that was featured in several episodes of the program. (A zipline is a rope with a pulley on it that stretches between two points, and people ride on the pulley.) "A zipline would be great to have on the roof of my treehouse for an escape route," I told my friend David. I scavenged an old rotted piece of hemp rope and stretched it precariously from the top of my treehouse, high above the field below. I tied the other end of the hemp rope to a huge old fir tree. To my surprise and delight, I discovered an old wooden pulley in a pile of junk behind the garage. It looked like something that had come off a big old pirate ship. Among the junk I also found a piece of cast-iron pipe. Crudely tying the hemp rope around that iron pipe, I created a handle for the zipline. Then I attached a heavy string to the handle so we could hoist the pulley to the roof of my treehouse. When we had finished the project, we tied our zipline securely to a branch.

Lying on our backs, we tipped back a bottle of Coca-Cola, and gazed up at our handiwork. We played on the zipline a lot.

Several days passed. David and I were up in my treehouse one day when my dad walked out of the house. He noticed me playing with the zipline. "Hey, don't fall out of there and break your arm," he shouted.

"Oh no, Dad, I won't," I replied.

Don't bet your life On a broken-down wooden pulley

Dad drove off to work. I started arguing with David to see who was going to be the first to ride the zipline. When I realized David was winning the argument, I jumped up and grabbed onto the handle. In a flash I was zipping backwards! I couldn't see where I was going. Fear hit. I worried about the possibility of smacking into the tree at the far end of the line. Suddenly, I swung in midair and something broke loose. I was shocked. In my mind, I screamed, "OH, NO, I'M FALLING!!! HERE COMES THE GRRRRROOOOUUUOUND!!!!" I stiffened my body before I smashed into the ground, landing on my feet. Thud!! My hands were up over my head, holding onto the heavy iron handle attached to that rock-hard pulley, both of which simultaneously slammed onto my head.

The momentum caused me to fall forward. I swung my hand around to protect myself. My hand hit the dirt so hard I snapped the outside carpal bone. My hand was twisted 180 degrees on the end of my arm.

My face smashed down into the dirt, my nose crushed flat as a pancake. In a state of shock, I stood up. I brushed myself off with my one good arm and gazed down at my crooked arm. Something was drastically wrong. However, I didn't feel any pain. I curiously studied my arm. I knew something was haywire because the arm wasn't on straight.

I straightened both arms out in front of me. One of my thumbs pointed down toward the ground. The other one pointed up at the sky. "This doesn't look right," I said out loud. I moaned. Still, I didn't experience any pain. I hobbled over to the fence. The instant I grabbed hold of that fence, ready to climb over it, the pain hit me. It was excruciating. "Something is definitely wrong!" I muttered. I wrapped my arm up in a chunk of the Sunday paper and tied the whole thing together with black electrical tape. My sister and grandma drove me to the emergency room of the local hospital. I was laid up in that hospital for three days with a cast from my hand to my shoulder. From that day on I developed a monstrous fear of heights. The greatest fear I would ever face in my life was all triggered by that one disastrous plunge from my home-made zipline.

When I got home from the hospital, I made an inspection of the zipline. I was amazed to find that the rotted hemp rope had not broken. The pulley itself had broken apart and that was what had caused me to fall. This inspection was my own personal quality control.

After that tremendous fall and painful injury, it was almost impossible for me even to climb a ladder. My father asked me to do some repairs on the roof of the garage.

Mastering Fear: The Ultimate Challenge

I set the ladder up, but when I stepped onto the first rung, my body froze because of fear. I experienced the feeling of falling, although I was only standing on the first rung of the ladder. I pushed myself through massive fear and climbed onto the roof. I was terrified once I was actually up there on the roof. I knew I had to get back down after I completed the repairs. I trembled at the thought of stepping over the edge of that one-story roof. I spent about an hour up there worrying about getting off that roof rather than doing the job.

Years later, I got a job that helped me overcome my fear of heights. I spent two weeks as a roofer on a 20-story skyscraper in downtown Seattle. There were no safety belts. It was 20 stories from the top of the roof to the concrete sidewalk below. The perimeter of the building had only a 12-inch curb to keep me from falling. I realized that if I walked too quickly toward the edge, I'd plunge to my demise on the sidewalk 20 stories below.

My first day on the roof of that 20-story building, I was just petrified with fear. I crawled on my belly, worming my way over to the edge of the roof. Peering over the edge of that 12-inch curb, I could visualize my body actually falling. I experienced a vision of falling and hitting the sidewalk. I worked to choke back my tears. Ego wouldn't allow me to bawl in front of a group of macho construction people. It was all I could do to keep from crying. All day long I was thinking, "What the hell am I doing here? I can't do this! This is crazy! I'm going to quit!"

Despite my distress, I showed up and worked that job for two weeks. To my amazement, after those two weeks I could stand on that roof with very little fear.

The day we finished the job, I stood on top of that 12-inch curb around the perimeter of the building. Without a safety belt on, there was nothing but thin air between me and the sidewalk. I stared 20 stories down without batting an eye. My imagination no longer projected a movie of myself falling and splatting onto the sidewalk below.

Here I was, standing on the roof of a 20-story building without fear. The gods had smiled on me, and I was given victory over my fear of heights. How did it happen? I don't know. I had no conscious intention of mastering that fear—it just happened. Without conscious intention, I spontaneously mastered my worst fear. I'm not saying that I don't experience fear of heights; I now have a different perception of it.

You gain strength,
courage, and confidence
by the experience
in which you really stop
to look fear in the face.

You must do
the thing
you think
you cannot do.

Eleanor Roosevelt

3

HANG GLIDING PROVED TO ME THAT FEAR IS IGNORANCE

One day a member of Challenges Unlimited, Inc., (referred to in this book as "CU") walked up to me and said, "Hey, Steven, why don't we go hang gliding?" That pushed my buttons and brought up a lot of fear. Specifically: fear of death, fear of falling, fear of heights, fear of flying, fear of the unknown, fear of gravity, fear of trees that impale hang gliders, fear of mother earth coming up too fast and smacking hang gliders like flies with a fly swatter, etc. Just a normal everyday range of fears.

I watched people hang-glide off Mount Si near North Bend where I used to live. I marvelled. I said to myself, "That's pretty neat. You'll never get me up there flying around on a piece of cloth with a little bit of aluminum frame. *I have no need to do that.* Those crazy fools can do that all they want. I admire their courage, or their stupidity, whatever it is that makes them do it, but I don't want to do it." The real reason I didn't want to hang-glide was that I was afraid. There were two reasons I was afraid: first, I had a lifelong fear of heights and second, I was afraid because I didn't know anything at all about how hang gliding was actually done.

Mastering Fear: The Ultimate Challenge

When I admitted I was afraid of hang gliding, I became curious. I decided to get some information about the sport. I realized from firewalking that the best way to overcome fear is to face it head-on. You have to "take the bull by the horns." Fear has a way of haunting you forever if you refuse to face it. I didn't want fear to limit my life. I recognized it was time for me to go hang gliding. The most logical way for me to do that was to familiarize myself with the equipment and find out exactly how it worked. I needed to get the facts, to understand the risks and potential dangers associated with hang gliding.

"How big do you think the kite's wings are, Steven?" a friend asked me.

I replied, "Uh, about 12 to 14 feet. The rig is perhaps only about six feet long. It's really quite small." I had seen a couple of pictures of hang gliders. I attempted to project the actual size of the hang glider from my impressions of the pictures I'd seen. Watching hang gliders soar 2500 feet above me in the sky, it was extremely difficult to judge the size of the glider. I couldn't figure out how people could get themselves into that cocoon where pilots seemed to hang in space below the glider frame.

My expectation of hang gliding was that if I jumped off a launch pad from a 1500 foot-high mountain, that would be all she wrote. I would surely fall out of the sky and plunge to my death. Something would inevitably break; something would go disastrously wrong. I was informed by my buddy that the actual wingspan was about 38 feet. "Oh, really?" I said. I began to understand that the size of the glider rig was a lot bigger than I had assumed.

I thought riding a hang glider would be comparable to riding on the back of a mosquito. It appeared to be more like a glide on a 747 by comparison to what I had imagined. This is an example of how knowledge changes perceptions of the world.

Ignorance can scare the daylights out of a person. People are afraid of the dark because they don't know what's out there. I had no idea the wings were that big. I explained, "I don't think I have enough experience to launch a hang glider by myself off a 1500-foot-high cliff." My friend informed me it wasn't necessary to do all those things by myself. I would be making a tandem flight with an experienced, certified instructor. He would facilitate the process and give me detailed instructions. The tricky and dangerous takeoffs and landings would be done for me by my instructor. All I had to do was to run off the mountain when he said run.

I started pumping my friend with questions. "What if the instructor weighs more than I do? Won't it make the glider fly cattywampus? Will that cause the glider to list to one side? What happens if we go into a spin?" My friend laughed. His response was that both the instructor and the student hang from a central pivot point on the hang glider. They form one centralized payload on the glider. That gives the glider a great deal of stability.

"The instructors must be light, then, huh?" I asked.

My friend responded, "How much payload do you think a hang glider can carry?"

I replied, "Ummmm, 350 pounds?"

His answer surprised me. "Seven hundred pounds."

We talked for an hour and a half. I exhausted my friend, asking every question I could possibly think of. I began to understand that my beliefs about hang gliding had been misconceptions based on ignorance, not on reality. After I received that information, I searched out a qualified and certified tandem hang gliding instructor and enrolled in a class. A few weeks later, I went hang gliding off a 1500-foot mountain! It was one of the greatest experiences of my life.

When you consider doing something potentially dangerous like hang gliding, look for a qualified instructor who has all the proper credentials. Make sure he is certified by the governing authorities of city, county, and state. See that he has all the proper licenses and insurance and that he belongs to a professional association. Check his reputation with others who have used his services. Get the best training, study, and learn as much as you possibly can. It's far safer to study from a qualified master than to risk your life with an amateur.

Fear Is Ignorance

Fear is an illusion. It's much like watching a magician. The magician makes an elephant disappear, pulls a rabbit out of a hat, saws some lady in half, or appears to burn money. The magician is well aware that he is creating an illusion by means of distracting the attention of the audience from what's really happening. Magic happens when distractions catch the eyes of the observer. The observer is ignorant of what's really happening.

When you pay attention, you become aware of all the factors involved. Then you understand the real risk factor involved in an activity. You realize that negative projections and imagined disasters are usually based on fear and ignorance.

There is no fear in love
Love casts out all fear

I John 4:18

4

GO JUMP OUT
OF A PERFECTLY GOOD AIRPLANE

When you live in the Northwest, you can expect to spend a good deal of time preparing yourself mentally for a parachute jump. There's an abundance of rain in latté land. It's against the rules to jump when it's raining. Two members of Challenges Unlimited were committed to skydiving. On a Wednesday, the three of us drove to the airport to take the class. We arrived at the airport and received instructions on how to jump properly out of an airplane. Is there any "proper" way to jump out of an airplane? Yes, definitely. It's no fun to plunge to earth upside down at 130 m.p.h., so it pays to follow instructions and do it right.

Jumping out of an airplane is a natural thing to do if you pay good money to buy a ticket. When you're two miles high over mother earth with a parachute on your back and you are in to MasterCard for about $200, jumping out seems like a logical way to get your feet back on terra firma.

If you don't jump, you lose your money. Not only that, you lose the experience. You lose your self-esteem and you realize you're "yellow," a true "chicken." Oh, well. That's okay. There'll always be another plane. However, it gets harder and harder to follow through and take action each time you chicken out. This is the price you pay for not following through.

I had been invited to go parachuting a number of times during my lifetime. Before I walked on fire, I'd say, "No way!" My standard line was, "Yeah, I'd like to go do that but I've got such and such an obligation. . . ." I made up excuses. I was terrified of heights.

A lady brought parachuting to my attention one day. "Steven, I think it's time we went parachuting. Let's just go do it!" she said. A few days later, we were on our way to the airport. Once again, I felt like a condemned man. I asked her if I could have one last request. Could I please have breakfast at the airport? After all, this might be the last day of my life. Soon I would fall out of the sky, my chute might not open, and I might hit the ground at 130 m.p.h. They wouldn't even need to bury me, the hole would be so deep! They could just throw dirt clods in my face and put a modest wooden sign over my grave with my name, date of birth, and the date of my death. *Here lies poor Steven. His chute didn't open. He should have stayed home.* I thought about that over my ham and eggs. Boy, did that airport food taste good, even though I had a mighty queasy stomach.

We paid for our tickets. We all got adrenaline rushes. We were primed and pumped. We were disappointed when the staff told us that the weather was so lousy we wouldn't be able to jump that day. We had to take a rain check. Ahhhhhhh . . . saved by the rain!

Two weeks later, we weren't allowed to jump because of the weather. Two months later, we weren't allowed to jump because of the rain. How was I supposed to get killed if they wouldn't even allow me to jump out of the airplane?

We finally went back to the airport on a day when the weather was just perfect. We skipped work and headed for the airport.

I had butterflies in my stomach as the little Cessna lifted off the ground. I saw the earth receding below me. The cars, buildings, and roads were shrinking, shrinking, shrinking. I had an altimeter strapped on my chest. I became increasingly concerned and uptight as I watched that blasted altimeter. It read 1000, 2000 feet, then 3000 feet. The higher we got, the more scared I got. It only takes 15 to 17 minutes to get up to 12,500 feet in this dinky little airplane. The engine noise vibrates the plane outrageously. I thought the Cessna was going to blast apart and come unglued from the vibration. You can't even hear yourself scream at the top of your lungs.

I looked at the inside of the plane. I shouted, "Hey!! It looks like some of the screws are loose in this plane!!"

"No!" the pilot yelled. "They're missing!! Some of the screws fell out!"

My instructor motioned for me to put on my goofy-looking goggles and a pathetic, thin little leather helmet. What good would a 1/8-inch-thick cowhide helmet be if I hit the ground at 130 m.p.h.?

Mastering Fear: The Ultimate Challenge

We were cruising at 10,000 feet. I realized I only had a couple of thousand feet before jump time. That translated into eight to ten minutes before they would open the door of the airplane. I whispered a prayer. I knew I was about ready to plunge to my death.

There we were, a cameraman, the instructor, the pilot, and I. Fear totally kicked in when my instructor grabbed my harness and hooked me to his harness. A great, secure feeling. Even the pilot had a parachute, and I was the only person in the plane who didn't have a parachute! It seemed like there was no turning back.

When you do a tandem jump, you have no parachute. Your instructor is the only one wearing a chute. If you were to come unhooked from your instructor in midair, it would be curtains. You would impact the earth at a speed of at least 130 m.p.h. At that point, the instructor looked out the window and said, "Okay, okay, okay, let's check it out."

Here I was, scrunched down on the airplane floor, which vibrated so outrageously it felt like a tornado was ripping it apart. I was down on my hands and knees right next to the door of the airplane. The instructor screamed, "Okay, it's time! Open the door!" He opened the door of the plane about a foot. The wind blasting into the plane felt like 140 m.p.h. My eyes bugged out! I looked down and saw the ground. It really seemed crazy at that point. It was just nuts. I couldn't even see buildings, cars, roads—nothing. They were all invisible. Disappeared, vanished, they were all so small. That's how far up we were!

Everything was gone except for major landmarks: earth, sky, lakes, and mountains. Everything else was too microscopic even to see! You'd have to have a telescope to see the airport from that high up!

"This is crazy, absurd, this is totally INNNNSSSSSAAANNNNNEEEEEE!!!" I thought. I glanced over to the dashboard in front of the airplane. I focused my attention on the instrument panel with all its little dials, gizmos, and gadgets. I had to do something to distract myself from the horrific thought that I could fall out of that little hole, the open door of the airplane. I felt absolutely sick. However, when my instructor actually opened the door all the way, I didn't experience any fear. Only when the door was open part way did I panic. "I could accidentally fall out of that little hole at the wrong time, plunging to my untimely death," I thought.

Suddenly the airplane door opened all the way. Out flipped the cameraman. He threw his body out and hung off the wing strut by his two hands. The cameraman poised himself, preparing to jump in sync with us. My instructor looked over at the cameraman. "Ready, set, GOOOOOOOOOOO!!!" He roared so loudly, I could actually hear him. I bailed out. I pushed off real hard like superman, arching my body. I was falling! WOWWWWWW!!!!! Away I go!!! That plunge is such an adrenaline high that some people experience sensory shutdown. You can actually black out for a second or two. I don't recall being upside down. When I watch the videotape, it's evident we "turned turtle." We were upside down until we stabilized. I must have been in a partial blackout at that point.

We plunged straight toward the earth. We were falling like a rock, straight down at a speed of 130 m.p.h. Gravity was doing a wonderful job. If I didn't know I was falling, I could have sworn I was flying. We continued to arch our backs. We spread our arms. Soon we cruised back into correct position. We were falling with our center of gravity, our bellies toward the earth at neck-breaking speed. After 60 seconds of freefall, the chute opened with a tremendous "pop" and we decelerated from 130 m.p.h. to five m.p.h. in three seconds flat. We popped the chute at 4000 feet. That was a lot of G-force exerted on my body through the harness I was wearing. The instant we popped the chute, I was acutely aware of two little straps, digging into my crotch with a vengeance. The only things saving my bacon were those two nasty little straps ripping into my crotch.

We slowed down tremendously. We drifted across a friendly, lazy sky. "You wanna play?" my instructor asked.

I was so relieved that the chute had actually opened and I was still alive. Play sounded fabulous. It beat lying dead in some field, flat as a pancake. I didn't want to miss out on some mid-air turns and a stall. Not after I had just taken a death-defying plunge into the unknown from 12,500 feet and actually survived it. "Yeah, I'm up for it! Here we are in the moment. Let's go for it. ROCK AND ROLL!!!" We did a couple of grand sweeping turns one way, then some graceful sweeping turns the other way.

"Hey, you wanna do a stall now?" my instructor asked. When you stall out with a parachute, you come to a dead stop in mid-air. You pull down on both tethers that control the chute and that causes it to stall. You hover in mid-air for a minute. No movement up, down, or sideways. It's just like putting on the brakes.

You only stay there for about three seconds before the canopy of the parachute collapses. Then you fall backwards. The chute refills with air, but it's one scary drop through thin air before that happens. We did a stall at 3500 feet. It was like being injected with pure adrenaline.

When we were falling at 130 m.p.h., I felt a terrific blast of air going in one nostril and blowing everything out my other nostril. When I landed on the field with my instructor, both of us were wiping snot off our faces. I couldn't tell if it was from my nose or his nose—it didn't matter. It was revolting, disgusting, and plain embarrassing, but it didn't matter, because we had an exciting adventure! Here we were with our feet on solid ground. What a rush!

The second time I skydived, we jumped through clouds. The FAA says you're not supposed to do that. Jumping through clouds is a real trip because you have a reference point that allows you to see exactly how fast 130 m.p.h. is. It was one astonishing ride. Extremely quick.

I expected to experience the sensation of falling the first time I jumped, but there really was none. Jumping on a clear day was like staying stationary in the air because you have no reference points to show you how fast you're moving. It's like you have an enormous fan blasting at you at 130 m.p.h. coming up from the earth. We dove out at 12,500 feet. From that altitude, it would take about 70 seconds until impact with the ground if the chute didn't open. That's a long time to freefall. The experience of skydiving is different from bungee jumping in that sense. You experience a tremendous feeling of falling with the bungee jump, but you only fall a couple of seconds before you have a gigantic bounce-back. You're hooked to a giant rubber band, which is the bungee cord.

My skydiving experience rewarded me with a realization about life and death. Diving out of an airplane is a leap into space that helps you master your fear of heights. Skydiving, like bungee jumping, is a leap from the known into the unknown. Skydiving is a magnificent way to confront both the fear of heights and the fear of the unknown.

I'm convinced that fear of the unknown is the greatest fear we face in life. Fear of the unknown is born entirely out of ignorance. Facing fear of the unknown is the hardest thing most of us will ever do. Once you face the fear of the unknown and master it, you're free.

The first time you do something is always the scariest. It makes the strongest impression on you. I will long remember vaulting off that airplane wing strut for the first time. The sun was a dazzling yellow streaked with gold. The sky was royal blue. There was not a cloud in the sky. Gazing to the south, Mt. Rainier looked like an upside-down snow cone. I could see the entire cityscape of downtown Seattle stretching out like a patchwork quilt. I peered downward toward the ground with the wind screaming in my ears. I could calculate the exact spot where I was going to collide with the ground if we didn't manage to get the chute to open.

It was bizarre. I was swept over by a peaceful feeling of composure. It was like waves of the ocean coming over me. Complete acceptance assured me that even if the parachute didn't open, I *knew* that I would be okay, *even if I died*. In that moment of bliss, I would have been able to observe the entire experience of "death" without horrific thoughts. At that moment, I felt that God was completely in charge of the universe, because I knew that I had no control over the outcome. God was taking care of it all. If I bit the dust, I could watch and experience, enjoying it all the way and feeling completely safe. I was reminded that there is love and order in the universe. There's a higher power running the show.

When we fear the unknown, we're afraid something will go wrong. Skydiving, bungee jumping, and walking on fire are all less dangerous than driving a car, and we drive our cars daily. We're afraid that things are out of our control. When you skydive, you realize that in reality, things actually are out of your control. You might as well accept it. When you do that, you'll get a great feeling of peace and serenity. You won't become overly serious about life. Everything is going to be okay, anyway. Things will be all right. They always have been and they always will be.

Problems are created in the mind. Fear of the unknown is created by the thoughts of the mind.

We only create what we give energy to. When we fight with thoughts, we energize them. Once the thoughts are accepted, they lose their power and the fear is gone. Mastering fear makes love possible. Plan right now to master your fear. Decide right now to go skydiving and *DO IT!!!* Skydiving is a tremendous way to overcome not only your fear of heights, but also your fear of the unknown.

"Terror turned into joy, fear into love and trust. I bounced around below the bridge, swinging free and easy like a baby being rocked in a cradle by his mother. I was alive, I didn't die, and it was FUN!!!!!!!"

5

HIGHWAY TO THE DANGER ZONE: BUNGEE JUMPING!!!

One day a member of Challenges Unlimited, Inc., brought me a full-color brochure advertising a bungee jump. "Hey, Steven, here's a new challenge! Look at this bungee jump. You can jump off this 140-foot bridge with one of these giant rubber bands on," he said excitedly.

"Not me," I thought to myself. I sat down and examined the brochure with nervous excitement. "This is crazy," I said out loud. I realized, however, that I couldn't pass judgment on the bungee jump, no matter how insane it seemed, without doing it first. In spite of my fears and insecurities, we set a date to go bungee jumping.

At that time, none of the members of CU had bungee jumped. We were all pretty excited and somewhat terror-stricken at the prospect.

We thought it would be good to begin to prepare ourselves mentally to jump off a 140-foot bridge. We began to visualize what the experience would be like. We pictured ourselves standing on a bridge 140 feet above a river. We projected emotion into our visualizations, and soon we felt like we were living through the experience in advance. I could only do that for about three days.

Picturing myself on that bridge poised to take the plunge, I experienced a real emotion of terror. Three days of that was enough self-torture.

The visualizations actually produced an adrenaline rush. My mouth went dry, my stomach twisted, and I got butterflies. My heart pounded and beads of sweat broke out on my forehead. The palms of my hands turned cold. All this was my body's reaction to a visualization of jumping off a bridge with a bungee cord tied to my feet. I began to think about my experience of falling from the zipline when I was a kid. After three days of this, I was at my wit's end. I refused to think about it any more. I shut off my imagination and waited for the day to arrive. When the big day came, there was an ominous feeling in my living room where we all gathered at midnight. At 1:00 o'clock in the morning, we were watching a video of the bungee jump and making decisions about the order in which we were going to do our jumps. Scary? You bet! But it was also tremendously exciting. We set off in the middle of the night for the six and one-half-hour drive it would take to get to the bungee jumping site. Enthusiasm was high. We were all saying, "Let's go for it!!!"

We arrived the next morning bleary-eyed at the bungee jump. Rolling into the parking lot, I'll never forget seeing the most massive wood and steel staircase I have ever seen before or since. "Hey, wait a minute! I think there's been a mistake! We must be in the wrong place; let's go home! I didn't realize that I'd have to climb to my death!!" I didn't plan on that at all, but that's exactly what went through my mind. Several of us were saying the same thing at once. I got out of the car and climbed up that huge cold steel staircase onto the bridge. This was about

45 minutes before the bungee jump opened for the day. Craning my neck, I gazed over the railing of the bridge. By visual calculation, it appeared to be 140 feet down to the river.

I had never actually seen anyone jump off the bridge except in a video. There was no way the video could do justice to the perspective you get when you're standing on a 140-foot bridge ready to jump off. A cord was wrapped around my ankles as I waited to be the first jumper of the day. The set-up crew was arguing about whether or not the counterweight was properly set up. This severely shook my confidence and filled me with insecurity. "What else is wrong with this setup?" I thought. "Maybe they even forgot to tie the bungee cord to the bridge!" They grabbed my arms and helped me shuffle out to the edge of the gangplank. I couldn't see a bungee cord. Where was it? It was hanging out of my line of sight underneath the bridge. I wondered if the cord would break.

When I got out on the gang plank, I looked down. My perception of that bridge height doubled instantly.

"Hey, are we hooked up???" I shouted.

"Yes, you're hooked up!" the operator replied.

Suddenly, my perception was that I was 280 feet above that river without a bungee cord on. *Fear overwhelmed me. I panicked!* My mind started screaming, "I'm NOT doing this!!! No way am I jumping off this bridge!!!!"

At that moment, it seemed I was staring death right in the face, committing suicide. I was jumping off a bridge without a bungee cord, plunging down 280 feet to splat into the river. "You're going to fall off this bridge. You're about to die," my mind was babbling. I could see a gravestone with my name on it. A modest stone, no frills.

Just my name, date of birth, date of death, and the inscription: *Here lies poor Steven. They forgot to hook up his bungee cord.*

When you're jumping off something that high, your rational mind tells you that *you're not going to survive*. Period. End of story.

My mental plan was to count down: five, four, three, two—one. On the count of one, I would jump. I turned around to the operator. "Will you count for me? Give me a countdown." It felt like the last request of a man about ready to be hanged.

"Well, of course," he said cheerfully. "Are you ready?"

"Yes, I'm ready," I replied. He half-shouted a rapid countdown, "Three, two, one!" I nearly collapsed and grabbed hold of that railing.

"Now wait a minute," I said, "you need to start at five, and on the count of one, I'll go."

He replied, "Okay. Are you ready?"

I shot back, "Yeah, I'm ready."

He quickly counted, "Five, three, two, one."

My knees buckled and I almost fell off the bridge. I grabbed the rail again. That wasn't part of my mental plan. My programming was five, four, three, two, one—jump. He had skipped the number four, which threw me off kilter. "Okay," I said with the energy of irritation, "this time don't skip any numbers!"

"No problem," he said and went into another countdown. "Five, four, three, two, one."

My body responded and I jumped. My mind went berserk and screamed at me. "You stupid S.O.B!! You just jumped off a bridge!!!" Visions of Wile E. Coyote (the cartoon character who continually falls off cliffs) flashed in my mind. I craved to get back on the bridge one more time but alas, it was too late, I had just jumped to my death! It was too late now. "It's only a matter of seconds until you'll be SPLATTTTTTTTIINNNGGG ON THAT WATER DOWN BELOW!!!!" My mind roared.

I was hurtling through the air with a tremendous rush of speed.

Time slowed down. It nearly stood still.

I felt a loud rush of wind through my hair. Suddenly, it was as if there was an angel grabbing me by the ankles, slowing me down. I was safe!! I didn't have to die. The bungee took effect. Thank you, God! Thank God, I can still live! What a relief!

Whatever the fear is take action and move past it

Instantly, I was feeling intense joy—pure ecstasy—bouncing over a hundred feet on the end of a giant rubber band. I was attached to a bungee cord after all, sort of like a giant umbilical cord, saving me from death. In the wink of an eye, fear became excitement. Terror turned into joy, fear into love and trust. I bounced around below the bridge, swinging free and easy like a baby being rocked in a cradle by his mother. I was alive, I didn't die, and it was FFFUUUUUUUUNNNNNNN!!!!!!!

After I quit bouncing, I hung by my feet. Then I was lowered into a big rubber life raft. A guy unhooked me from the bungee cord. As the boat took me back to the shore, I realized that the entire process had taken only about three and a half minutes. Blood rushed to my head and I felt a bit faint, but I was ecstatic. Bungee jumping taught me an important lesson. If I choose to, I can take action in spite of horrendous fear.

All the thoughts surging through my mind as I stood on the gangplank had been negative. I could only see death below me. But the actual experience was joyous, powerful, and extremely positive. This was a result of being able to step through fear and ignore negative visualizations.

It's better to jump and die than not to jump at all

Steven Bisyak

I had high enthusiasm. I wanted to help the 11 other members of my group conquer their fears and jump. I wanted them all to experience what I had experienced.

When I got back on the bridge, a lady was having her ankles wrapped and getting ready to jump. I told her my experience had been well worth it. I wanted to do it again. She didn't need help or encouragement to get off the bridge. She had her mind made up. She had mentally programmed herself and decided that if I did it, she'd do it. She wanted to do a swan dive. We got a video of her doing a beautiful swan dive off that 140-foot bridge.

Next, it was time for another lady to jump. This particular lady had a lifelong terror of heights. She couldn't even stand on a chair in her kitchen without holding on to the cupboard. She would lose her equilibrium. In spite of her fear of heights, she parachuted twice before she bungee jumped. I admired her courage.

She was anxious to get it over with. She worked her way out onto the gangplank. She felt a noticeable weight from the bungee cord pulling on her ankles, like her feet were being pulled over the edge of the gangplank. Suddenly she yelled, "Hey, I'm not doing this!" and started backing off the gangplank.

I got her attention and started talking to her immediately. I reminded her of her accomplishments, the things she had successfully done. I mentioned her firewalking—something that was "impossible," but she'd done it many times. I reminded her about her skydiving experiences. These were major accomplishments she'd already successfully done.

She admitted that skydiving had been a blast. I was encouraged. I wasn't going to give up on her. I gave her a pep talk. As I told her I believed in her, she began to listen to me. Soon she edged her way out to the end of the gangplank. She kept looking at me as she did so. "It's okay," I said. "Just move. Take action. Go. You didn't drive all night long to come up here and deny yourself from doing what you want to do. You've waited for this moment for a long, long time." Her stated intention for the bungee jump was simply to have fun.

About a quarter mile down the canyon, a train came to a stop on the trestle spanning the river. People in the train intently watched the woman through their binoculars. They took pictures of her as she stood on that bridge, poised and ready to jump.

She was thinking to herself that if she jumped off the bridge, she would die. For her, the bungee cord was irrelevant. It wasn't part of her reality at that moment. At that instant, she made the sign of the cross, and she's not even Catholic. She stood on that gangplank for about ten minutes before finally deciding to go.

Suddenly, she fell off the bridge. She screamed one long AAAAHHHHHHHHHHHHHHHHHHHHHAAA-HHHHHHHHHHH!!!!!! at the top of her lungs. Instantly, she was in the canyon below the bridge, bouncing and swinging in huge arcs on the end of the long bungee cord. She wailed and hollered for about a minute and a half, until she finally grabbed a contact pole and was lowered into the shuttle boat. The train let out three long "WHOOOOOOOOO, WHOOOOOOO, WHOOOOOO's," and began to chug away.

A couple of months later, her housemate watched in amazement as this same woman did a tapdance on a chair in her kitchen. Imagine that! She had such a terror of heights, she couldn't even stand on a chair before bungee jumping. Afterward, she did a tapdance on a chair. Her perception of heights had changed. I was surprised and happy to hear that she had purchased a ticket to do a second bungee jump.

Extreme Measures Create Extreme Change

Steven Bisyak

Another lady had an experience that was different from most of ours. She had no fear at all as she stood there on the gangplank, bungee cord tied to her feet.

"You want me to count down for you?" the operator asked.

She replied, "No, I want to do it all by myself. Just let me do my own thing." She leaned back, rolled up her sleeves, got set, and jumped. There was no fear at all until she launched her body into space. Then it was like pure terror. She had never experienced hysteria, fear, and horror like that before. "What did I just do!! I FORGOT TO CHECK MY EQUIPMENT!!!!!" She was fearless until after she jumped, going into a state of shock until the bungee took effect.

One by one, nine out of the 11 people in our group dove off that bridge that day.

I loved the experience and I wanted to do it again. In addition to the tremendous rush, I learned so much about myself, standing up there on that bridge. Bungee jumping is a plunge from the known into the unknown, especially when you've never jumped off a bridge before. At the same time we were mastering our fear of heights, we were mastering our fear of the unknown and having an absolute blast doing it!

Several weeks later when I bungee jumped a second time, I was dealing with my fear of being on the *Geraldo* show.

Geraldo was preparing to tape a show called *Geraldo's Believe It or Not*. Geraldo invited Tolly Burkan to do the segment on firewalking. There would be other guests on the show, including Dr. Andrew Weil, the author of a number of books. Geraldo asked Tolly to locate someone who could perform body piercing for the audience. Jack Schwartz was a possibility, but he was not able to schedule the time. Tolly knew I had done body piercing in the past, so he asked me if I would do it. He also asked if I would do a segment on brick breaking. The show was to be broadcast nationwide before an audience of 30 million people.

I was extremely excited at the prospect of being on national TV, particularly on a show about something that turned me on as much as firewalking. Excitement turned to sickening fear when I realized what that really meant. Not only would I be on TV in front of 30 million people, I was supposed to run a five-inch doll needle completely through my hand without pain and without blood.

> *Confront fear in one area of your life*
> *by doing something that*
> *requires courage*
> *in another area of your life*

I had no fear of jumping off the bridge the second time. I dealt with my fear of falling on my first jump. My fear of being on the *Geraldo* show was far greater than my fear of jumping off a bridge. Here's one of my secrets for overcoming fear. I was using my fear of jumping off a bridge as a metaphor for my fear of being on *Geraldo*. Fear is just fear, period. It's the same fear—whether you are asking for a job, asking for a date, confronting a problem, or giving a speech.

I was afraid to run a needle through my hand in front of 30 million people. What if it hurts? What if I hit a bone? What if it bleeds? What if I make a fool of myself, and can't do it? The bungee jump was something new to me and was still mighty scary. I figured it would be a great metaphor, representing my fear of being on *Geraldo*. Although firewalking is always scary, it didn't inspire terror as much as the bungee jump did at that time in my life.

I couldn't be on *Geraldo* until I actually boarded the plane and flew to New York. However, I could throw my body off a bridge with a bungee cord tied to my feet to powerfully represent my fear.

Create metaphors for yourself. When you successfully master fear in one area of your life, it carries over into all other areas.

If you're serious about victory over fear, if you're serious about success, you can use these physical challenges to create the quality of life you want. Mastering fear means removing limitations. Do you want to become unlimited? Are you willing to accept responsibility for the quality of your life?

As a result of my experiences, I've learned that confronting fear in one area of your life can help you overcome it in another. Put your fear into something immediate and tangible—for instance, a bungee jump. If you're afraid of asking your boss for a raise, go bungee jump first. It does wonders for your self-esteem. Asking for a raise might even seem easy compared to jumping off a bridge with a bungee cord tied to your feet.

*A journey of a thousand miles
begins with a single step*

Old Chinese Proverb by Who Flung Poo

6

A PULLEY SWING
AND "SUICIDE RUN"

The Pulley Swing

In chapter two, I related a story about a fall I took when I was a kid. I fashioned a crude zipline that went from my treehouse across a field. The pulley broke, causing me to take a painful tumble onto a field with a pulley crashing down on top of my noggin.

The pulley swings I build today are quantum technological leaps from the crude zipline I invented when I was a kid. Money is no object when it comes to investing in gear and equipment. I use high-quality, industrial-grade equipment, including 10,000-pound test wire rope, high-test stainless steel pulleys, and mountain climbing gear designed to withstand far more stress and strain that just one person's weight.

When I purchased five acres of land in North Bend, I had a lot of trees to play with. My first adult pulley swing was about 200 feet in length, sloping downhill. I built a wooden footbridge at the top, which puts you about 12 feet up into a tree. Before you launch into thin air, you have to climb a ladder, which is about five steps, the last one of which is nothing but a thick piece of wire. You have to keep your balance with one foot while you put your other foot out into space and then into a loop of rope. You have to keep that one leg straight as you jump out into space. The entire run only takes about four seconds from the top to the bottom, so it's definitely a quick ride.

There are two ways to ride this swing. At the top of the rope are two handholds. You can hold on with your hands while you put one foot in the loop. Another way to ride is to have a body harness on. Then you're hooked to the rope. I guarantee you're not going to fall off the swing with your body in a harness. The only problem is, when you get to the bottom, someone has to come and get you with a 12-foot stepladder, which wobbles a bit on my steep hill. That can be scarier than riding down with one foot in a loop. It's also scary to have just one foot in a loop, 'cause if you let go, it's crash and burn on the hillside.

So how does it stop? It stops by gravity. When you get close to the bottom of the ride, the rope slopes upward into a tree. You don't quite reach that tree before gravity pulls you down again. After rolling back and forth, you come to a complete stop in about four seconds.

The pulley swing is about 30 feet off the ground. To get down off the swing, you pull your weight off your foot that's in the loop, then let yourself come down the rope hand over hand until you reach the ground. You have to hang on tight or you'll get a nasty rope burn.

The pulley swing is a great adrenaline rush, the first time you do it. After the initial fear wears off, it's still fun and exciting, but the first time is special. So relish it, because you get the greatest rush the first time you ride it. You'll never be quite that afraid again.

The Suicide Run

The suicide run is a modified pulley swing with a unique twist to it. It's much steeper than the pulley swing, for one thing. You jump out of a tree, and the angle of the wire is about 45 degrees. You're almost falling as you make this jump. It's a wicked angle, extremely steep. Fortunately, you have a harness on with a bungee cord attached to your back. Before you hit the tree at the far end of the wire rope, the bungee takes effect and you're pulled back. There you go, bouncing back and forth until you come to a stop.

What will we do when the excitement of riding these swings eventually wears off? I suppose we'll just have to build bigger and better ones. How about a suicide swing over Niagara falls? Five thousand, no, 10,000 feet long. If that's not long enough, we'll hook one end to the tip of Mount Everest and the other end to the Statue of Liberty in New York Harbor and. . . .

With these swings, you only have to take one little step, but that first step can be a real doozie. Whether you are jumping off a bridge or a crane doing the bungee jump, or out of an airplane skydiving, or off a pulley swing, you have to take the first step. Once you take that step, you usually lose your fear. Then fear becomes excitement, and you can really enjoy the experience you create by taking that first step.

7

THE ROPES COURSE

One day a friend came to me with an idea he'd come up with after seeing the movie *Medicine Man*. "Steven," he said, "we ought to do a ropes course right here on your property. In the movie *Medicine Man*, they had to hunt rare and exotic herbs and plants that grew way up in the trees in the South American jungle. They did it by using ropes and pulleys to move from one tree to another. It looks like it would be a good challenge for people, and a way they could learn to trust themselves."

I believe the biggest benefit of the ropes course is that it does teach a person to trust and rely on himself. You're harnessed in, and you have a main rope and a safety line. At each point where the rope is fastened to a tree, there's a changeover point. You have to make sure that you very carefully and methodically change each pulley over and that you always have one of the lines supporting your weight. If you're not paying 100% attention, you could fall 30 to 40 feet to the ground. It doesn't take brute strength, but it is a mental and physical challenge, especially if you're not used to using mountain climbing gear.

The ropes course is one of those challenges that gives you a great feeling of self-confidence after you've done it. It's a gentle ride, and it's perfectly safe if you're paying attention.

8

FALSE EMOTION VERSUS REAL EMOTION

All negative emotions and the problems created by them are based in fear. All positive emotions are based in love.

For example, assume someone's spouse or significant other has lunch with an attractive person. Then imagine that his or her mate finds out about this luncheon after the fact. The spouse didn't tell his or her mate. In a case like that, there's a good chance there will be some jealousy. The reason is because the spouse or significant other went out to lunch with an attractive person without first communicating with his or her mate. In a situation like that, it would be natural to feel jealousy or even anger. Anger is only the byproduct of an underlying emotion of fear. Insecurity causes the anger, and insecurity is a mild form of fear.

Let's consider a few examples of this:

SITUATION	RESULTING EMOTION	UNDERLYING EMOTION
Husband, wife, or significant other has lunch with an attractive friend of the opposite sex.	Jealousy; feelings of rejection or anger.	Lack of trust; fear of loss of relationship; fear of abandonment.
The boss says, "I need this job done right now," when the employee already has too much to do.	Frustration; irritation; feeling under pressure.	Fear of criticism; fear of job loss.
Child disobeys the parent's instructions and runs out in the street.	Parent is upset; angry.	Fear of injury or death to child.

What can be done about it?

SITUATION	REALIZATION	ACTION
Husband, wife or significant other has lunch with an attractive friend of the opposite sex.	Realize there is an underlying lack of trust and fear of losing the relationship. Upset because somebody else is receiving all the attention. This is why people feel jealous and resentful.	Love and trust are the answers. Actions based in love; forgiveness needed; open communication with spouse is needed. Allowing instead of controlling.

SITUATION	REALIZATION	ACTION
Boss says, "I need this job done right now," when there is too much to do already.	Understand there's an underlying fear of criticism; there is a fear of loss of job.	Communicate with the boss and let him/her know how you feel. Ask for help in setting priorities. If the worst happens and the job is lost, it may not be all that bad. Things always have a way of working out.
Child disobeys instructions and runs out in the street.	Fear of the child being injured or killed.	Need to regain composure quickly; act rationally and focus on getting the child out of danger; then discipline with love.

Ego is not the enemy.

Jess Guess

9

EGO

Ego is that part of the self that likes to get recognition. It loves to be stroked and petted. The ego's job appears to be keeping us separate from one another. When you firewalk, you get in touch with your ego. If you're walking to show how great you are, and paying attention to other people instead of what you're doing, you can get burned. Thoughts like, "I wonder what she thinks of me" or "I wonder how this is coming across on the TV cameras" cause you to lose your focus and you can become distracted. When that happens at a firewalk, you can fry your feet quicker than greased lightning. It makes a believer out of you when you quick-fry your feet just by losing your focus for a second.

The ego is a part of us. I don't think people accomplish much in this world without it. Some people have given it up. They're the ones who go veg out in a cave for 50 years. I'm not condemning that, by any means. To each his own.

Ego can actually get you to the firewalk. You hear about a friend firewalking, ego starts talking to you and you say, "If he did that, I can do that too!" So you go to the firewalk to prove you're just as good as the other fellow. Then, once you get to the fire, it's time to get out of ego and pay attention to walking safely on the fire. Fear kicks in when you actually face the fire. When you get to the firewalk, you don't want to be consumed by your ego. The function of the ego is over once your foot hits the fire.

From time to time we become aware that we have an ego. Sometimes we judge it as bad. If it's bad, we think we're not supposed to have it. We want to destroy it, get rid of it, or crush it. We might enter into a "wrestling match" with it, which only makes it harder to get rid of. Ego, like fear, serves a purpose. If it's in balance, it serves many good purposes.

I tell people at the firewalk to avoid being show-offs. Yet the desire to impress can get the best of you, and that can get you burned. Burns often occur when you put others before yourself. Life can "burn you" too. That happens when you pay more attention to other peoples' responses than to what's going on inside you.

Can you keep from being burned by life? Probably not, but every time you get "burned," you can learn something. Life is a series of lessons. Ego can destroy relationships if it leads to too much selfishness. It can destroy the quality of a person's life. It needs to be in balance. When ego runs riot, it's out of balance, out of control. It can turn negative and destructive.

When you firewalk, you don't know what your experience will be until after you've crossed over the fire.

Perhaps you'll feel no temperature. You may blister; you might even burn. You don't know until after you've done it. Ego leads people to try to predict the results of their actions. When you give up ego, you give up predicting the results of your actions.

Inappropriate expectations might set you up for disappointments. If you don't expect much, you will likely be happier and more satisfied with the results you actually achieve. In other words, you'll be pleasantly surprised! When you firewalk, you allow the forces of nature to meld with your life force. You become one with the fire and one with nature as you confront your fear.

Taking your shoes and socks off at a firewalk is a commitment to the experience. If you follow your inner guidance, energy takes over and gets you across the fire safely. If you take too much credit for your experience, that can be an expression of ego. You have to allow yourself to go with the flow.

Practice letting go
of your ego

Ghengis Kahn, *from his letter to*
Alexander the Great, advising him to
"be more humble"

Sometimes experienced firewalkers learn lessons by getting blisters or burns. You can never quite predict how or when this is going to occur. Ego tells you that you can firewalk because other people can do it. That may be true, but you can never precisely predict the results of your experience. If you could, there would be nothing left to learn and nothing left to burn!

When you firewalk, you're usually pleasantly surprised, relieved, and delighted to discover you feel no heat in the coals. Occasionally you do get a blister or a burn. When that happens, you might search for answers. "Why? Why me?" It's hard on your ego, especially if you're the only one who gets burned that night. It brings your ego into balance. The firewalk can teach a lot about the ego. It can remind a person of the need for humility.

Ego is self-centered thinking. Ego says, "Hey, everybody, look at me! Here I go; watch me walk on fire!" That idea can get you a nasty burn, because you're not focused. You're not paying attention.

Webster defines *ego* as:

> The self, especially as contrasted with another self or the world.

Egoism is:

> A doctrine that individual self-interest is the actual motive of all conscious action; a doctrine that individual self-interest is the valid end of all actions; excessive concern for oneself. . . .

Ego-tripping is:

> An act or course of action that enhances and satisfies one's ego.

Ego is closely related to fear. Ego is what you experience when you're afraid of burning yourself. That's a confession that you're firewalking on your own steam, walking by self-will. You've taken on 100% responsibility for the *results* of your firewalk. It's useful to have a healthy respect for the ego. Ego is like the red light on the dashboard of your car, warning that the brakes are on. Obviously, you don't want to move the car until you take the emergency brakes off. You also don't want to step into the fire until your ego is in check.

When your mind is focused on walking on fire, it's best to let go of an egocentric attitude. You can only pay 100% attention to one thing at a time. You're either into ego or into a focused mind. Take action only after the ego is under control. You'll discover, "Yes, that did work." Or, "No, that didn't work." Experience is the greatest teacher.

I allow myself to feel the ego, experience it, and then let go of it. I admit my fear; it's just another part of being human. It's sad to realize how much fear and ego inhibit and block our lives on a day-to-day basis.

Overcoming fear involves taking risks. The more you do this, the more you'll master your fear. Ego needs to be brought into balance; you don't need to kill it. Nor do you need to kill fear. Just bring these parts of yourself into balance through actions coming from love. Start with your self; begin by loving yourself. That makes it possible to love others.

As the ego loses its grip, you'll still have fear. The difference is that you'll no longer deny the ego and the fear. Ego thinks, "I'm soooooo cooooooooool!" It says, "Look at me. I want to IMPRESS you. I want to look good. Aren't I GRRRREEATTTT???? Watch me!!" So you vainly try to impress others. Somehow it never seems to pan out. It doesn't quite come off the way you thought it would. Instead of the praise you're looking for, you get insults. Instead of a cool experience, you get a nasty blister or a burn. Not a lot of fun. Then you get angry or depressed.

The way we live our lives is a response to our structured beliefs. If you've been living in ego, you've been reacting a lot. Life hands us many choices on a daily basis. Think about your options.

Freedom from ego and fear is real freedom. You no longer have to react automatically. You're free! You have a choice. When ego and fear no longer rule your life, you're free to consider your options and respond in a functional way, a way that works well for you personally. If your ego gets the best of you, and you react, don't beat yourself up with the club of guilt. Just "get back on the horse." Life will soon throw you another baseball, so do your best and take another swing.

10

SECRETS OF ENERGY

There have been times in my life when I had too much to do. For instance, clearing my property, building my house, negotiating to construct a bungee jump in San Diego, putting together 75 bungee cords for eight bungee jumping sites around the nation, running Challenges Unlimited, Inc., being a facilitator for Firewalk Instructor Training, and doing corporate training for a branch of the nation's largest corporation. All of this within a period of four weeks.

That series of jobs required me to work 20- to 23-hour days. I averaged from one to three hours of sleep per night during those four weeks. One of the reasons I was able to do that is because I've learned how to conserve and use energy.

In my opinion, the way energy works is a process of flow. It seems like if you start thinking about it, you interfere with it. For example, it's like saying to your friends, "Hey, watch me walk on fire." It's something you just don't talk about. It can't be contrived. It has to be spontaneous. You have to just do it.

Using available energy starts with a feeling, but it's directed by thought.

Here's a powerful key to how it works: the more emotion you pack behind your intention, the more your energy will accomplish. You'll be more effective.

You have the ability to shift mental gears. You can use your emotions in a way that can benefit your use of energy. Just as you shift gears in a car, you can shift your mind-set to get the results you want. The stronger the emotion you put behind a desire, the more it accelerates the energy. The result of this is that you can accomplish a lot more in your life by a conscious use of this technique. Just shift the gears of your mind. Visualize yourself successfully achieving whatever it is you want to accomplish. Then step on the "gas pedal" of emotion to get the results you want. Infuse emotion into your visualizations. Feel the thrill of accomplishment as you picture yourself turning your dreams into reality!

Think about a fighter for a moment. A fighter trains to put out a lot of energy to win a fight. You can train yourself to use your emotions so that you will become more like a fighter. You can train yourself so that your body will automatically respond the way you want it to.

Your energy is like a mirror. It's a reflection of what you hold in your heart. Your heart contains a lot of different emotions, not just the emotion of love. It contains everything you desire to bring into reality, all that you want in life. That includes all your aspirations, good and bad, your hopes, your dreams, and your desires.

When you begin to use energy, you need to realize that it's a force and that you can create through your actions. Sir Issac Newton said, "For every action, there is an equal and opposite reaction." The Bible says, "What you sow, you will reap."

What you see manifested in your life is a reflection of your mental condition. If you're getting a lot of anger from those around you, it might be that you're putting out a lot of anger. Send a negative emotion, and you might get a negative response. You get back what you put out. If you want to bring more love into your life, start by giving love. Give what you most want to get back. If you want more energy in your life, put more energy out.

For example, money is only stored energy, or a symbol of stored energy. If you want more money in your life, begin to give out more energy. You will begin attracting money. Some people think that they have so many irons in the fire, that they can't get it all done, and they think they'll never accomplish anything. Don't limit yourself! You can do far more than you ever thought possible. Throw more logs on the fire!! You want more money? If you want more money:

Put Another Log on the Fire!!!

How long has it been since you last rode a bicycle? If you have ever been on a bicycle, it doesn't matter if it's been one year or 20 years, you'll still remember how to do it. Most of us are aware of these principles of energy, but we forget. When you begin using energy, it seems like it comes with its own rules and it's own principles or "cookbook."

Energy is sort of like a computer. You turn on the computer and that energizes it. You probably know what its capabilities are. You've done this so many times that it's almost like you're on automatic pilot. It's ingrained in your cellular structure, so it's automatic. You don't have to pick up an instruction manual and read it. As soon as you turn the computer on, you intuitively know how it works and how to use it because you've done it hundreds of times before. Energy is like that.

Sometimes we send, as well as receive, negative energy. I'm aware of both positive and negative uses of energy.

I first learned about energy in early 1980. Conscious and unconscious uses of energy come hand in hand with the responsibility for the use of them. However, they've never let me down when I've used them consciously, in a positive way. The laws of energy, as well as gravity, work without fail.

You can change the programming in the "computer" if you're getting an undesirable response. For example, if you find yourself in an undesirable situation, for instance a bad job or a bad relationship, you can use energy to your advantage. If you begin using energy in a positive way, you can turn things around in your life. Working with energy can help you turn negative experiences into positive experiences.

Life is a series of lessons. There are lessons to be learned from all the actions we take, positive and negative. An example of this is learning a lesson about energy when you hit your hand with a hammer. It really gets your attention. When you do that, you know that your energy was misplaced and perhaps you aren't paying enough attention.

Love has been called an emotion, but it's also an energy. There are many kinds of energy, and they produce different results. You have a specific energy, I have a specific energy, every human being has his or her own energy. All things have energy. Einstein said that matter can neither be created nor destroyed, it can only change form ($E = MC^2$). We can learn how to draw and attract more energy, and how to utilize that energy to create the results we want in our lives. We have unlimited energy available to us. How are we using that energy?

Another way you can use energy is to draw upon the available energies that are all around us. You can "grab" energy that's in external things around you and use that energy in conjunction with your own.

Belief is the Beginning of All Accomplishment

Where there is a will, there is at least one way. For example, if you want to pick up something that's heavier than you can lift, draw the energy from a tree, a rock, or the air, anything that's close around you. It's like a "contact high." If someone around you is energized, is "pink and has long ears and keeps on going," like the Energizer Bunny, he or she can inspire you to keep on going! Focus that energy. Make sure your intentions are clear. If those around you are negative, bummed out, and depressed, they can bring you down, and it's hard to stay enthusiastic. So choose and use your energy wisely!

A lower energy can't penetrate a higher energy, but a higher energy can penetrate a lower energy. Fire is a constant energy. If your energy is extremely high, then the energy of the fire cannot harm the firewalker. If the firewalker is coming out of an emotional state in which his energy is extremely low, then the energy of the fire is greater than that of the firewalker, which results in blisters or burns. However, the excitement generated when you walk into the fire can *instantly raise your energy*!

During my firewalking workshops, I often tell stories about people who experienced burns in the fire. That generates a lot of excitement or fear. I don't do that to torture the class; I do it to help them raise their energy. That helps them get safely across the coal bed. If you have a task to do, raise your energy! Get motivated and focused to accomplish your intentions.

Determine what result you want to create. Focus on your intention, 100%! Once you make a decision to do something, take action and go for it! Don't think about it, just do it.

When you get down to basics, there's really nothing as powerful as the power of the mind. I encourage you to begin using the visualizations and then start consciously using energy the way I've described in this chapter. Then, watch and enjoy the results.

11

FUN WITH SPIDERS AND SNAKES

I was talking to someone who had a lifelong phobia of spiders and snakes. His mother grew up in Wyoming, where rattlesnakes and black widow spiders lived under the front porches of houses. When his mother was a little girl, she used to kill them by beating them to death with a shovel.

"When I was a kid," he explained, "my mother used to scream whenever she saw a spider or a snake. Even if it was a harmless snake or a harmless spider, she would scream hysterically. If she could catch it, she would kill it. When my mother screamed, I became hysterical because I thought she was being hurt or killed. She would do the same thing whenever she saw a mouse or a rat come into the house."

"I remember one time," he continued, "when my brother terrorized my sister with a huge brown spider he found downstairs. My sister screamed and cried as he tortured her by pushing that big brown spider into her face. There was a great deal of fear in our family around spiders and snakes."

The other night I had a dream about a snake. Actually, I was the snake in my dream. I was inside the snake's body and in its mind. As the snake, I was lying on my belly in a field of soft warm dirt and I became aware that there were humans around me.

"I had love in my heart for people. I was a snake, yet the nature of my heart was to love people. The people didn't notice me at first, but when they finally did, they became very fearful."

"I didn't even try to escape because I wanted to be near these people that I loved. I was lying there serenely blissed out by the thought that there were humans all around me, when suddenly a huge boot came crashing down on my head. The people that I loved so much were killing me as quickly as they could, stomping the life out of me. I realized that they were killing me because of fear. I was lying there, with the life force ebbing out of my body. My heart was filled with love for the people who were killing me. Love overshadowed the pain of my body being killed. I was sad and sorry that people didn't understand the love in my heart. In spite of being killed by them, I only loved them more. In the dream I was the snake. After having that dream, I wonder if it's possible that snakes have feelings, too."

All his life this person had been taught to fear the snake. He had killed snakes with shovels, had crushed spiders, and once he actually uncovered and killed a whole little family of innocent field mice with a shovel. Our reaction to spiders and snakes is all out of proportion to the real danger.

He went on to tell me that he had never been hurt by a snake in his entire life, even though he had killed many of them. The only time he had ever heard of anyone being bitten by a snake was when the person had stepped on the snake, scared or injured it, or even tried to kill it. Only then did the snake bite in an attempt to protect itself.

Why did he react this way to snakes? He learned it from his family. Fear of snakes is learned. It's not a fear we're born with. Psychology teaches us that we find "scapegoats" to keep from feeling our own guilt and shame. We project evil onto a person or an animal. In that way we separate ourselves. We then feel that evil is not a part of ourselves, not realizing that evil is potential in each one of us.

People such as Hitler, mass murderers, people who commit crimes of all kinds are our teachers in a negative sense. If we didn't have such people teaching us that negative actions bring pain and suffering, we might be doomed to do those things ourselves out of ignorance.

I had a pet python named Detroit. Detroit was like one of the family. He really enjoyed getting out of his cage, being held and stroked, and he loved being around people. He was about 13 feet long, weighed about 80 pounds, and was completely harmless. I took him to elementary schools and the children handled him. Depending on his mood, we liked to bring him out during the firewalking seminar, so people could confront their fear of snakes. Once people realized he wasn't going to hurt them, they could see him for what he was. Snakes really can make nice pets.

I also had a pet tarantula who enjoyed getting out and being with people. That tarantula never hurt anyone. We've had camera crews filming as people would let it climb from hand to hand. Even the kids got to handle him.

Once you learn something about the habits and nature of animals, you realize that many people have a lot of misperceptions and needless fear because of ignorance.

12

HOW TO BREAK BRICKS, BOARDS & ROCKS— WITH YOUR BARE HANDS!!

Brick Breaking

Breaking a brick with your hand is done by using the same mental techniques as walking on fire, body piercing, or bending rebar. It involves clear intention, mental focus, paying attention, and taking action. I usually use a type of brick called red Roman brick that's available at masonry outlets on the West Coast. You can break other types of brick, but some are harder to break than others. I wouldn't recommend using concrete reinforced brick until after you've mastered some easier kinds of brick.

Elevate the brick to a height of 25 to 30 inches to allow enough space between the brick and the floor so you don't slam your fist into the floor after you break through the brick. For example, create a brick stand by using two 50-gallon drums as supports for each end of the brick. Place the brick between the two drums or use two wooden chairs to support the brick over the floor. You should have as much of the brick exposed as possible. Only 1/8 inch to

1/4 inch of the edge of the brick should rest on the edge of the drum or chair.

Intention

Your intention should be clear: to go completely through the brick, not just to hit the top of the brick. If you intend to just hit the top of the brick, that's all you'll do. You might get a sore hand that way, so make sure you intend to go completely through the brick so that your hand will end up about 12 inches below the brick after you hit it. Practice placing your hand below the brick to see what it feels like to have your hand at your destination, where your hand should end up.

What's the worst that can possibly happen if you take a swing at the brick? It might not break? You might break your hand? You might sprain your wrist? Allow yourself to get in touch with your own negativity, and take a look at it. If the worst happened, could you accept it? The answer to that question should be a clear "yes" or "no." If the answer is "no," then you have no business hitting a brick with your hand. You're not willing to take the risk of a negative outcome yet. Another example of this is, if you can't accept the risk of a car accident, you have no business getting in a car. But if your answer is "yes," then you're ready to let go of all your negative thinking.

Ask what's the best that could possibly happen if you hit the brick. A clean break, with no pain felt in your hand. You might feel empowered! It could change your life! You would be able to accomplish more than ever before!

Now, you're ready to take action. Let go of every negative thought you had concerning the outcome. Focus only on the best that could possibly happen. Your hand is about to go completely through the brick.

Pay Attention

What should you pay attention to?

Pay 100% attention to your intention which is: to go completely through the brick

Paying attention means letting go of every distraction and completely focusing your mind on what's before you. Look at the brick. See your destination, 12 inches below the surface of the brick, and picture your hand ending up there. Paying attention means that the only thing in your mind is your intention, going completely through the brick.

If you have the slightest negative thought or doubt, you won't go through the brick. I know from experience that it's a lot less painful to break the brick than it is to hit it and not break it. I have seen people "try" to break a brick and literally beat their hands on the brick until they were black and blue. Put an item on the table in front of you. Try to pick that item up. **Don't do it, just try to do it.** What happens? Are you successful in accomplishing what you want to do?

If you picked the item up, you didn't pay attention to the instructions. If the item is still sitting there, erase the word "try" from your vocabulary. There is no such thing as "try." You either do it, or you don't do it. You either jump or don't jump. You either walk or don't walk. The success is in 100% commitment and not in 98% commitment.

Believe in yourself 100%. Know that you can break the brick. I've seen an eight-year-old child do it. Believing in yourself is an excellent attitude to carry into everything you do in life.

Be willing to forfeit your hand. Make your hand an extension of your mind, and your hand will become a tool for you, like a hammer. I make it look easy because it is. However, I'm not always successful, either, if I'm not paying attention. These principles don't discriminate. They are laws of energy, and they don't care if you are a millionaire or you're dead broke; they don't care if you're a corporate executive or a street sweeper. They'll work for you if you apply them. The brick doesn't know if it's your first one, or if you've broken a thousand bricks before.

Once your intention is clear, to go completely through the brick, focus your mind. Let all other thoughts and mental chatter go. Picture a crack in the middle of the brick.

As you swing on the brick, realize that it's crucial to sacrifice your hand. Just give it up. If you're not willing to take a risk on the worst possible outcome, injuring your hand, then you have no business swinging your hand full force down on a brick. You have no business asking for a raise if you can't accept the possibility of getting fired. If you can accept the possibility of a negative outcome, focus on the best that can possibly happen for you. Think of what this will do for your self-confidence. Sure, you can do it!

Put emotion into it! Think of something that makes you angry, if that's what you need to do. You can convert your anger or energy into action and break the brick. It works! Put your full body weight into that swing, and don't hold anything back. Sacrifice your hand. Make believe your hand is a hammer, if you like. Commitment is the price of success and the brick can teach you a lot about commitment.

Here's an important thing to keep in mind when you break a brick. When somebody gets in an automobile accident involving a drunk driver, who usually gets injured? The sober person usually gets injured. Why? Because the drunk is too relaxed to get injured.

A person can get hurt breaking a brick because his or her arm and hand are too stiff and rigid. Some people tense up because of fear. So before you swing down on the brick, just relax your arm.

If you follow the directions above, the brick will break, and you'll end up with your hand at your intended destination, at a point 12 inches below the brick. You might discover that it's so easy, it's almost unbelievable. The most important thing is to take action and go for it 100%.

The bricks are excellent teachers. If the brick doesn't break, it should become a fantastic teacher for you. I've learned more from the bricks I didn't break than from the ones I did break. If you hit the brick and it doesn't break, you're not a failure. It takes guts just to step up to the brick stand and take a swing on a brick. If the brick doesn't break, you'll inevitably ask "why," and in answering that question, you can learn a lot about yourself.

Once I was asked to teach a woman to break a brick in front of 30 million people on the *Geraldo* show. I picked a young lady named Debbie out of the audience. Debbie was about 25 years old and had a very slight build. I could tell by her enthusiasm and energy that she would be the one to break the brick. We went backstage.

I had never met Debbie before. The first thing she told me when we got backstage was, "I walk on fire." That was an incredible coincidence!

I said, "Debbie, this'll be a piece of cake for you. It works exactly like the firewalk. There's a lot of fear associated with doing this, right? If your intention is to break the brick, you'd better pay attention 100% to breaking that brick. What's the worst possible thing that could happen?"

Debbie replied, "What's the worst that could happen? The brick might not break, and I could break my hand in front of 30 million people."

"Okay," I said, "Take that horror thought and let it go. What's the best thing that could possibly happen?"

"I might break that brick without breaking my hand, without pain," Debbie replied.

I told her to make a mental picture. "Debbie, you really want to break the brick. Put your emotion, your desire into it, 100%. That's the key. What's the best that could possibly happen? Focus on the best and then take action. When you feel you're ready, just do it. GO!!!"

Within four minutes, I taught Debbie how to break a brick, and she broke one backstage. When we came out in front of the audience and cameras, Geraldo asked, "Debbie, do you feel ready?"

She replied, "Definitely."

Geraldo turned to a young man in the audience. "Do you think she can do this?" he asked.

"No way," the young man responded.

"Why not?" Geraldo asked.

The young man replied, "She's too small, she hasn't had martial arts training, the brick is too thick—it's solid—and that smile doesn't look too intimidating. There's just no way she's going to do it."

The audience was ecstatic to watch Debbie's hand slice through that brick like a knife going through butter. The videotape shows what a thrill it was for Debbie to do that. Debbie broke her second brick in front of an audience of 30 million people. Was she ever ecstatic!

Once I prepared to break five bricks in front of TV cameras. I swung down on them with my whole body weight and all the force I could muster. On the first hit, I fractured the bones in my hand. That was a shock to my system, but I was determined to succeed. I continued to pound and pummel those bricks with my broken hand. After I pummeled them again, they began to break, a couple of bricks at a time. I had to smash those suckers with my full force two more times after my hand was broken.

When I left the set, my hand was throbbing like a pulsating neon sign. My hand and wrist swelled up immediately. I realized my hand was no longer straight on my arm. It was a different shape, definitely not the configuration that I had known my whole life long, except that it looked like it did after I fell off the zipline. My intention was to achieve healing as rapidly as possible. I focused my intention 100% into healing that broken hand. Within one week, I was breaking bricks with that hand again. So much for paying attention to cameras, instead of paying attention to breaking five bricks! That demonstrates the price of not paying attention. What do you want? Intention means that you know what you want. It's extremely important that we are absolutely clear about what we want to create, because we are creators in that sense.

Three hits, five bricks, I'll never forget that. I don't know if I broke any of the bricks on the first hit. I just kept repeating in my mind, "break, break, break!" If you're completely focused, you can hit a stack of five bricks and they'll all crack in one hit.

Breaking Rocks

You can break a rock using the same mental techniques I just described for breaking a brick. With a rock, however, you may have to hit it over and over again if it doesn't break. When you're breaking a rock, you have to prop it up somehow. Each rock is different.

Place the rock with the edges on something solid. Use a couple of rocks for a stand, so the rock you want to break is supported on the edges, and there's room below the rock for your hand to follow after the rock breaks.

I start by picking out a rock about 8 to 10 inches across and 1 inch to 1½ inches thick. Then I prop it up on another rock securely so it doesn't bounce all over the place. Next, I take my hand, mentally prepare, and focus my mind. Then I start beating and pummeling on the rock until it breaks. The rock is so solid, sometimes it has a tendency to bounce back after I hit it.

I've hit rocks up to 70 times before breaking them. If they don't break after 70 hits, I "give them back to God." If a rock doesn't break, I just let go and put the rock back into the river. Then I say to the rock, "Okay, I'm giving you back to God."

Once I had some trouble breaking a rock. I beat on it for five months. That produces some pretty good hurts, followed by some good healing, when you beat on the same rock for five months. Finally, I got that one to break.

One day Rosie went down to the river. She sat down by a pile of flat river rocks. She had practiced breaking bricks, but she was getting tired of spending money on bricks and then destroying them. That's when she made a decision to go down to the river to break rocks. Rocks are free and it still amazes me to see a lady breaking rocks with her bare hands.

Breaking bricks and rocks is an exercise in focusing and commitment that applies to all areas of your life. Where fear limits you, the lesson of brick and rock breaking can teach you how to get beyond the fear through intention, commitment, and taking action.

Bend, Bend, Bend!

Buck Redface

13

BENDING STEEL REINFORCING BAR—WITH YOUR NECK!!

Bending rebar with your neck is done by using the same techniques as breaking bricks, walking on fire, body piercing, or asking for a job or a raise in salary.

The rebar I recommend is usually 3/8-inch concrete reinforcing bar used to reinforce concrete walls and floors. If 3/8-inch is unavailable, I use 1/2-inch. It usually comes in 20-foot lengths, which I cut into thirds, so I end up with three pieces approximately 6 feet 8 inches in length.

Just below the Adam's apple in your throat is a hollow spot in your windpipe above the breastbone. The end of the rebar is placed in that hollow spot. People have bent rebar with nothing over the end, but there is a chance of scratching your throat, because the end of the rebar is sometimes sharp and jagged after cutting. So I fold up an Alaskan dollar bill ($100) and put it over the end of the rebar. If you want to get fancy, you can cut a chamois skin or a piece of leather into about a 2-inch square and put that over the end of the rebar.

Just before I bend the bar, I put all my concentration into the center of that bar. I project my mind into the middle of the bar. It takes 100% focus and 100% concentration to put yourself into the right state of mind. I start thinking, "Bend, bend, bend." When my body starts to move, and I feel the bar starting to go, I feel a familiar sensation that's similar to what I feel when I step into the fire. I just walk. A couple of times my female partner and I attempted to *try* to bend the rebar between us. It was just before we were to do a demonstration on a TV show. She placed her end of the bar in the hollow of her throat. I put my end of the bar in the hollow of my throat, and there we were, looking at each other with that rebar between us. At that point we *tried* to bend the rebar. Oh, man, it just about killed me. Cough, cough, gag, hack, cough, gag, cough, cough! We realized at that moment that there's no such thing as a dress rehearsal when it comes to bending a piece of steel reinforcing bar with your neck.

We realized you can't pussyfoot around when you attempt to bend a piece of rebar with your neck. We went for it 100%. The bar bent, we walked forward, and we kissed—with a piece of bent rebar still braced in the hollow of our throats, wedged between us.

When I bend rebar, I don't lose my focus halfway through. Once the bar starts to bend, it's a cakewalk (piece of cake). Getting the rebar to start bending is the hardest part. Once it starts to go, there's almost no resistance.

We've never found bars that were so hard in the middle that nobody could bend them. Rebar is a type of mild steel. It's not casehardened, so it's potentially bendable. I've seen people attempt to bend rebar and fail. Five minutes later, they get extremely emotional or angry and come right back and bend the bar using the energy of intense emotion to accomplish the job. That points out the importance of putting emotion behind the intention. Emotion is energy.

The principles of rebar bending are exactly the same as the principles of firewalking. The intention should be to bend the bar completely in half. You should pay 100% attention to bending the bar. Take a long, hard look at the worst that could possibly happen. Almost everybody who has ever bent rebar with his throat has mentally pictured himself with a piece of rebar piercing his throat, sticking completely through the back of his neck. I've never seen anybody injured by bending rebar with his throat. Some people have bent three or more pieces of rebar at one time, and I heard of a man who bent 16 pieces of rebar all at once with his throat. That's the world record for rebar bending.

Once you realize your horror thoughts, take a look at them one by one and then just let go of them. Think of the best that could possibly happen. For instance, if I can bend a piece of rebar with my throat, what other things can I accomplish in my life that I previously thought were impossible? Focus on the best and pay 100% attention. When you're ready, just go for it.

I've seen a lady friend bend two pieces of rebar at once. It's essentially simple. Anybody can do it, if they follow the directions.

How long do I have to focus before the bar starts to bend? Usually no longer than three seconds. If we've got our heads together, it usually takes my partner and I only a couple of seconds to bend it. If it takes more than ten seconds, there's usually some minor mental adjustments that need to be made in order to make it happen.

Rebar bending appears to me to be very similar to walking on fire. If you walk on fire, it's your own energy getting you across the fire. However, if you do it with someone else, there's always a chance you'll get distracted by the other person. It works well if your timing is on and you're both in sync. Whenever you do anything with someone else, it's best to be coordinated in your efforts with the other person. The best way is to work together as a team. Both people have to be totally committed. It's something you can't "try" to do. You either do it or you don't do it.

One day a member of CU came by for a visit. He said, "What's this on the ground?"

I replied, "Oh, you haven't ever done the rebar?"

He said, "I saw a video once where they were bending rebar. I immediately said, 'No way, you'll never get me to do that. Heck, no! I have no desire to do that! Not me, with a rebar sticking through my neck!' I've been avoiding it for months. I have a great deal of fear around it."

I placed the end of the rebar against my hip. "Here, put the end of the rebar right in your neck, below your Adam's apple, in the weakest part, where it will go right through to your spine."

"No way!" he screamed.

There was no way he was going to bend a piece of rebar. He had just asked me about it, but he had his mind made up. There was no way he was going to do it. "I'll hold one end and put it against my hip so that it doesn't move. You take the other end of that rebar and stick it right in the hollow of your neck. Right where doctors do a tracheotomy, right in the hollow hole in your neck, up against your windpipe."

"Where it's real soft?" he asked.

"Yes," I replied. "I'll hold my end steady; I won't move. Then it's all up to you. You're going to have to walk to me on your own steam."

"Come on, Steven. No way is that possible. NO WAY!!!" There was a group of people nearby, so we walked over to them.

I said, "Do you think you'd like to do it now?" At that point, he made a decision to do it. His ego wouldn't allow him to refuse me in front of a group of his friends. I reminded him, "It's just another fire. It's exactly like the firewalk."

He responded, "Oh, okay." After he bent the bar, he couldn't believe how easy it had been! "He just looked at me with those eyes, those expectant, hellacious, unyielding eyes. How could I refuse?" It's amazing what fear will do.

You can use the same principles you use to bend rebar when you get into difficult situations in your everyday life. It's just another "piece of rebar." If it's a problem in a relationship, it's like a piece of rebar between the two of you. If you're committed, you'll realize that you'll go to any lengths to solve the problem and come together. You'll think, "Nothing's going to come between us. It's the same scenario as bending rebar. Relax, take a deep breath, go though the steps one by one, and you can have the same success. You can come together through problems in a relationship by applying the principles of bending rebar.

Now you've arrived at the point where you're bending rebar, you're walking on fire, you're breaking bricks with your hands, and you're not afraid to bungee jump, skydive, or rappel. Suddenly you want to go after jobs, ask for raises, start relationships—everything becomes simple.

You're inspired! Congratulations! You've come a long way, baby! Challenges become exciting when you know you have the tools to meet those challenges and achieve success.

14

FIREWALKING: *THE ULTIMATE TOOL* FOR MASTERING FEAR

*Man's mind, once stretched
to a new idea, can never return
to its original dimension. . . .*

Oliver Wendell Holmes

*We die a thousand deaths through fear . . .
Yet fear is nothing but an illusion*

I've seen dramatic changes take place in the lives of people after they've learned to firewalk. Firewalking is a dramatic encounter with fear. The definition of firewalking is: walking barefoot over hot coals, measuring about 1200° Fahrenheit, raked out into a bed of glowing embers.

All your life, you've believed that coming into contact with red hot coals will burn you. One night you decide you're going to walk on hot coals, so you do it, and you don't burn your feet. That experience can begin to short-circuit your belief system.

What else have you believed is true for you that isn't really true? If you can walk on fire, what else can you do? Walk through walls? Walk on water? Levitate? What limitations have you accepted in your life without question?

Frequently, when people are invited to a firewalk, they feel fear and choose not to come. Some people overcome their fear enough to go to a seminar and then end up actually walking on the fire. People who have been invited to a firewalk and refuse to come can benefit by learning something about themselves. Yes, they benefit, even if they never go to a firewalk, just by thinking about the idea and facing the fear! Firewalking is scary. It's a powerful tool for changing your life. Once you know the truth about how fear has limited you in your life, your life may begin to change. Firewalking is a way of inducing rapid growth into your life by giving you a dramatic confrontation with your own fear.

When you learn about how to change your state of mind at will, you can successfully walk on fire and overcome obstacles in your life that previously held you back. When you stand in front of a fire with the intention of walking, you'll undoubtedly feel an enormous amount of fear.

The fire may appear threatening to you. Dangerous. Scary. Perhaps even deadly. Then, as you stand there watching the embers, they might begin to twinkle and wink at you. Magically, the appearance of the fire begins to change before your eyes. It starts to look like a glowing bed of roses. Or a carpet of luminous velvet. It seems to be inviting you. The way you perceive the fire begins to change, allowing you to walk through your fear and walk across the fire. The coals may appear flickering like a sparkling bed of Christmas lights.

When that happens, it's an indication that your state of mind has shifted! Suddenly, you realize you're on the coal bed! You're not exactly sure how you got there, but suddenly you're walking on red-hot coals. You feel a sensation on your feet, but they aren't burning; you don't really feel any heat on the soles of your feet. Then, as suddenly as you realize you're on the coal bed, you're across the fire pit and your feet are on solid ground once more. What a rush!!! You've just done what you previously believed to be impossible. What does the coal bed feel like? If done correctly, it feels like you're Captain Crunch with Crunchberries.

Fear can be intense during your first firewalk. Every firewalk is a new experience. Experienced firewalkers may not experience terror at each fire, but there definitely is a tremendous respect and appreciation for the experience. Firewalking puts you in touch with your feelings. You definitely find out "where you're at." You might re-establish or strengthen your connection with a higher power. Another interesting benefit is your strong bonding with the group.

Until people have actually done it, they're usually terrified at the prospect of walking on fire. Your belief system tells you it's crazy—you're going to get burned. The court reporter in your head begins running videos that show you all bandaged up in a burn ward, sitting in a wheelchair with plastic feet.

The firewalk boils down to an exercise in trust. Trust, faith, belief, and positive thinking are all similar attitudes. Trust polarizes you in a positive way, so that you can achieve victory over seemingly insurmountable challenges in your life.

101

Firewalking forces you to go beyond previous limitations you set for yourself. You get to confront yourself and you have an opportunity to become honest about *your fears*. It's gut-wrenching. Most people try to avoid it.

There's no more denial of fear. Here's "where the rubber meets the road." No more kidding yourself and others. It's just you and the fire. This is your life. You can no longer joke around and say, "No problem. I can do that easy, no sweat." The fire is in front of you. There's no easy-chair speculation about what a brave person you are. Most people are scared out of their wits.

TAKE A STEP
LET FEAR GO

DON'T FIDDLE AROUND . . .
STROLL THROUGH HOT COALS

Emperor Nero

When you walk on hot coals, you transform fear into positive action. It's all a metaphor for your life. You can take the principles of the firewalking seminar and apply them directly to your life. You can even "take them to the bank" and use the principles of firewalking to make more money. Next time you go in to ask your boss for a raise, you can remember the fire. With the memory of successfully walking on fire in your mind, asking for a raise can be a real cool piece of cake.

You get ready to walk. Only this time it's not a stroll on hot coals—it's a walk into the boss's office. The bottom line is, it's much easier to confront fear and walk through it than to experience fear forever!

Once you stop denying your fear, you take back your power. Fear is not the enemy. It's a friend that comes up and taps you on the shoulder and says, "Hey! Pay attention." Fear has always been there and it will always be there. Fear is just an energy! Extreme measures create extreme change. Walking on fire is an extreme measure that can create extreme change in your life.

I started firewalking in 1984. Firewalking radically changed my life. I experienced terror the first time I stood in front of the coal bed with my shoes and socks off. It was the worst fear I ever faced in my entire life.

Previous to firewalking, I allowed fear to limit me and prevent me from doing what I wanted to do in life. I envied others who were achieving their goals. I used to say to myself, "I sure would like to do that some day." "Some day" never came because of fear. I was afraid that if I took a risk, fear would overwhelm me and I wouldn't be able to take action. Ego wouldn't let me do that. Deep down, I was afraid of failure. The more inhibited I became, the lower my self-esteem sank. I achieved less and less because I was stopped cold in my tracks by fear. I didn't believe in myself enough. Firewalking was the key that helped me believe in myself more. Self-doubt stopped me from confronting fear. I justified my behavior, excusing myself for not doing the things I wanted to do in life. I wasn't quite being honest with myself.

After I walked on fire, I experienced breakthroughs in all my relationships. I became more honest with myself and others. I was no longer terrified of confrontation. I've jumped out of airplanes, bungee jumped off bridges and cranes, and walked on hot coals. Doing those things can seem easy, like the cat's meow, compared to dealing with problems in a relationship. Most relationships are real "firewalks."

I'm more self-assertive now. On the job, I don't cower before employers. I express myself freely without being too afraid of what other people might think. When you face fears, you're much less likely to be pushed around, limited, or controlled by others. When faced with new challenges, instead of saying, "No way!" you begin to say, "Hey, that would be cool! Let's go do it!" Life is an adventure when you know how to turn your fear into excitement.

Life is a firewalk!

The firewalk has been a major tool in most of the dramatic transformations I've seen. One example that comes to mind is a young single woman who was living on welfare with her two toddlers. Her first firewalk was a jaunt across a 50-foot-long cinder bed of fiery embers. That's pretty unusual for a first-time firewalk. Most firewalks are no longer than 12 feet—20 feet at the most. When I saw this lady walk over 50 feet of hot coals on her very first walk, I was impressed. "This is a pretty gutsy lady," I thought.

As the months rolled by, she joined us for a number of other firewalks. She even attended the one in 1987 where we set the *Guinness Book of World Records* for the world's hottest firewalk. That was her last firewalk. I recall her saying she intended to take the principles of the firewalk and apply those principles to all areas of her life.

She went back to school and graduated from college with a 4.0 grade point average! She's no longer living on welfare. She's now happily married. She and her husband have three kids. Her transformation was remarkable. She went from being on welfare to graduating from college with honors. She didn't let fear limit her. She had the courage not only to think about walking on fire, she actually did it. Then she applied the principles she used to walk on fire to create the life of her dreams. She put more in to life and she got more out of life.

With long-term exposure to the firewalk, you realize that the firewalk is only a metaphor. A metaphor is an analogy in which one idea or activity represents another, something that stands for something else. Firewalking represents your life. We "firewalk" every day of our lives by facing fear and meeting the challenges life has to offer.

I've heard people say, "No, I don't want to do that." Later they change their minds and attend a firewalking seminar. Sometimes you hear people say, "I have no desire to do that. You won't get me to do that in a million years." In a firewalking workshop, people learn how to master their states of mind. When the mind is conquered, the emotions are in check and you can walk on fire. You can use the same techniques to achieve anything you want to achieve in life.

One of the biggest challenges I face is getting past people's fears and prejudices. Firewalking produces *RESULTS* in people's lives. Most people are so conditioned to fear the fire that they react when you bring up "firewalking." They aren't really listening because they're reacting emotionally out of fear and old programming. The key to the whole thing is an open mind, allowing for the possibilities. Techniques that allow people to walk on fire directly apply to achievement in all areas of people's lives. This book is an attempt to turn people on to the world of possibilities waiting for them at the firewalk.

*Whatever you can do, or dream you can,
begin it! Boldness has genius, power and
magic in it. Only engage and
the mind grows heated.
Begin; then the task will be completed!*

Goethe

The Fire of Transformation

*The Same Fire That Burns the Wood
Hardens the Steel . . .
Step Into the Fire*

15

INSIDE A FIREWALKING WORKSHOP

(What follows are conversations from various parts of a typical firewalking workshop)

Steven: If you say you're going to do something and then you follow through and do it, it's proof positive that your intentions were clear. Your actions were consistent with your intentions and you got results! However, if you aren't clear about your intentions, you're like a ship without a rudder. Without clear intentions, you blow this way and that. You blow hot and cold, and you'll never achieve anything! Your chances of hitting your target or achieving your goals are slim to none without clear intentions. Look inside yourself. Get in touch with your feelings. Ask yourself the question, "Why am I here tonight at a firewalking workshop? What are my intentions for this evening?"

Out of the veteran firewalkers who are here in this room right now, how many of you have ever been burned? Raise your hands. (All the veteran firewalkers raise their hands.) (Laughter.)

My intention this evening is to give you some tools to help you step through the fear you experience, not only in the firewalk, but in your everyday lives. I want to give you a resumé of experiences you can recall the next time you find yourself in a fearful situation. That's my intention for this evening.

You new people: Why would you want to come here tonight? Let's go around the room. I want each of you to state your intentions for this evening.

Bill   [Veteran firewalker] I'm just here to be in the experience, to firewalk myself, and to be available for whatever help is needed here this evening.

Diane   Hi, everyone. I'm Diane, and I firewalked once a couple of years ago. I'm a student. I spend a couple of hours each morning studying specific subjects. I'm very interested in learning how to control and use the mind. I want to learn the skills involved in the firewalk so that I can teach these techniques to others, especially young people.

Ted The reason I came is because I believe the firewalk is a powerful metaphor representing change in my life. The firewalk is scary and dramatic. I, too, want to teach people to firewalk so they can overcome fear and change their lives in positive ways. I believe that if I can learn to firewalk myself, I can master my fear and change my life for the better.

Mark The reason I'm here is to reinforce a positive belief in myself. I call it Self Power. It's difficult for me to hold on to a feeling of self confidence day after day. The firewalk has always been a powerful challenge for me. My goal is to become absolutely self-confident in all situations that arise in my life.

Jason I'm here to firewalk tonight. That is my intention. Firewalking is an exciting, unique challenge for me. I love to do out-of-the-ordinary types of things. It gives me great satisfaction to experience meeting challenges like this. If I can successfully do this, I believe I can accomplish other things in my life.

Lois I have walked on fire several times before. I keep coming back. I'm here tonight to work on some self-esteem issues. There are also some emotional issues I'm working through.

Terry   I can relate to what Lois just said. Two years ago I was dealing with self-esteem and emotional issues. I used the firewalk as a tool at that time. After walking on fire these past two years, I'm a different person. I'm here tonight to assist others. I also want to experience the firewalk for myself. I do this so that I can learn to pay attention 100% in the moment. Not to what I did yesterday, or what I'm going to do tomorrow.

Laurie   The firewalk is something impossible, and I've done it. There are other things in my life that are impossible, and I'm doing them.

Susan   I'm here to walk on fire to relax. Yeah. After over 100 firewalks, it becomes extremely logical to continue with it. You realize how much energy is released as a result of walking on fire. *It makes you feel good mentally, emotionally, and spiritually.*

Steven   She's been around for awhile. (Crowd laughs.)

Jeff   I'm here to enjoy myself. I intend to do whatever I can to help each of you look inside yourselves and find your own greatest potential. Each of us can see more of our own potential by recognizing it in others around us.

George   Each firewalk is different. I come here because I enjoy meeting positive people who want to improve their lives. I get really pumped after each firewalk; the enthusiasm carries into my work! Firewalking energizes me. That's why I keep coming back.

111

Mary   I'm here trying to answer the question, "Who am I?" I'm also a firewalking instructor. As a firewalking instructor, you realize that the fire never ends. To me, firewalking is learning, processing, and growing. I'm here to experience the next step, the next growth, the next process. I've seen some amazing things happen to people after they learned to firewalk. I'm here to continue to share and experience my own personal growth.

PAY 100% ATTENTION

Heather   The thought of walking on fire has scared me to death. I want to overcome that fear. I feel the firewalk will be a stepping stone for me. I want to master other things in my life, such as relationships. I want to step out of the fire into the fires of life that I've been avoiding. I want to put this knowledge and experience to practical use in all areas of my life, especially in all my relationships.

Steven   Perfect, perfect. I've walked on fire over a thousand times. I now realize that if I'm not accomplishing something in my life that I truly desire, it's because I'm afraid to do it. Once you recognize the fact that fear is the only thing holding you back, you have options. If you choose, you can take action in spite of your fears. All you have to do is let go of the "what if's." Visualize positive outcomes to all your hopes and dreams.

Now I'm going to give you an exercise in paying attention. (Steven pulls out an empty non-filter Camel Cigarette package. An empty cigarette package is given to each of the workshop participants.)

Look at these Camel Cigarette packages. Read the paragraph on the back of the package and count the number of occurrences of the letter "e." Remember, this is an exercise in paying attention. Remember this whenever you do something in life. Pay attention. We're not talking about casual attention or just half-hearted, 50% attention.

A paragraph on this cigarette package reads:

[The following is in fine print] Don't look for premiums or coupons, as the cost of the tobaccos blended in Camel cigarettes prohibits the use of them.

How many letter "e's" did you find?

Bill	I found nine.
Steven	Mary, how many did you get?
Mary	I have nine.
Steven	Mary has nine, Bill has nine.
Diane	I got ten.
Steven	A moment ago, we were talking about the importance of paying attention. I'll give you a formula that can predict the results of your firewalking experience:

100 minus the percent of attention you pay equals the number of blisters on your feet

For instance, if you pay 98% attention:
100 minus 98 = 2 blisters
What if you're only paying 50% attention?
100 minus 50 = 50 blisters!

So you see, we're not just talking about *casual attention*. I want you to pay 100% attention. Do it again. Count how many letter "e's" are in that paragraph.

Lois	Eleven.
Steven	How many?
George	Ten.
Jason	I still got Ten.
Steven	You're right, Lois, there are 11. Jason, how could you miss one the first time? Did you find out which one you missed? Which one was it?
Jason	I looked right over it. Now I see the one I missed, right there!
Steven	Which word was it, do you remember?
Jason	I missed the "e" in the word "the."
Mary	Most of us missed the "e" in "the." You tend to overlook it because it's so obvious.
Steven	That's right. We always tend to overlook the obvious.

Next, here's another example of how the brain reasons. Have you seen this before? (Steven holds up a horseshoe puzzle in front of the class.) Do you comprehend exactly what this puzzle is? The more you look at it, the more you say to yourself, "it can't be done." The same process happens whenever you experience fear. The mind gets "stuck" and it's impossible to see a positive conclusion or outcome to your problem. Tunnel vision limits your options. That's the main reason we say to ourselves, "I don't want to do that." Fear immobilizes the brain.

Fear is an emotion, like anger, that shuts down your reasoning ability. Let me give you an example of that. Let's assume that you have a friend named Sally who's been going hang gliding and bungee jumping every single weekend. You suspect she may have self-destructive tendencies, but you really admire Sally's courage, and she does seem to be having a ball!

A year goes by and you realize that Sally isn't hurting herself and she's not harming anyone else. You've observed Sally and you notice her personality has blossomed since bungee jumping and hang gliding. She now has a more positive self-image.

One day Sally says to you, "Hey, let's go hang gliding next Saturday." The only thing that would stop you from going with Sally and having a whale of a good time is your fear. What if we crash? Questions and doubts fueled by fear flood into your mind.

What mental process prevents you from doing the same exciting things Sally does? Whenever we feel fear, it comes along with questions of "what if this happens" or "what if that happens." Whenever you ask, "what if this happens" or "what if that happens," you have just accurately identified *the exact source of your fear.*

Fear never projects a positive outcome of an activity. We have to make a conscious effort to ask ourselves, "What is the best that could possibly happen?" We don't do that naturally. We have to learn it, practice it, and do it over and over again until it becomes a habit. It requires a conscious effort.

In summary, the only thing that stops you from doing an activity that you might enjoy, that would stimulate your personal growth and development, is fear. The only thing that holds you back and prevents you from accomplishing just about anything is fear. Jason, your hand is in the air; do you have a question?

Jason   Yes, I do. From what you're saying, it seems like what we have is an ability to consciously change our attitude from negative to positive. Are we "tuning in" to the negative or the positive thoughts that are attracted to us by this changing of attitude?

Steven   That's right.

Bill   I can really relate to what you're saying about the negative voices I hear when I feel fear. It may not always be a voice, though; it can be pictures or projections of negative outcomes. Could you talk a little more about this voice that "kicks in" when we feel fear?

Steven   Sure.   Where do your thoughts come from? Some are from your memory and others seem to come to you as if you were picking up a radio broadcast with your mind. Your memory contains the elements of who you are. This is your identity. It's a composite of your name, where you grew up, what you experienced, everything you know, consciously and unconsciously. For example, I'm Steven Bisyak, you're Diane Smith, and you're Jason Jones. A name identifies who you are, your family origins, and generally tells whether you're male or female.

The *court reporter* is that part of your mind that most closely relates to your fear. The court reporter tells you everything that's happening to you in a negative way. Any time you experience a scary situation, the court reporter starts to chatter.   It says things like, "Don't do that. Watch out!! Danger!! Danger!!" It speaks in negatives. It rambles and jives, and it can even start screaming and yelling at you.

At my very first firewalk, I was astounded to watch a lady walk on a 20-foot-long bed of coals. It was about six feet wide and four inches deep. I watched a seven-year-old boy and an eight-year-old boy walk across that blistering coal bed. The next thing I knew, *my legs were walking toward the fire pit*! The court reporter inside my head started yelling at me.

"WHOOOOAAAAA!!! You don't have any insurance! You've got to work tomorrow. What if you end up in the hospital??? What if YOU BURN YOUR FEET OFF???!!!!" The court reporter reports negatively on everything that happens. It always projects negative outcomes to your experience, based on the worst that could possibly happen.

Another inner voice we can all get in touch with is what I call *inner guidance*. Thoreau said, "Some men walk to the beat of a different drummer." We all have our own "different drummer," our own unique sense of inner knowing. If we become quiet and still enough, we can tune in and listen to our inner guidance. Part of your consciousness has intuitive knowledge. Sometimes it's called intuition. Sometimes it's called "following your heart." When you stand in front of the fire tonight, you'll have the opportunity to get in touch with your inner guidance. Nobody's going to push, pull, or shove you across the fire tonight. You can't pay us to do that. The motivation has to come from inside you. If you make up your mind to ask your boss for a raise, nobody's going to drag you into the boss's office. The will to take action has to come from within. You have to be convinced within yourself that asking for a raise is the right thing for you to do.

I emphasize inner guidance in the firewalking workshops, because if you use inner guidance it will help you make right decisions and take right actions in all areas of your life.

When you stand in front of the fire pit tonight gazing at the glowing crimson coals, you might hear a still small voice say, "Focus. Go for it. Take action." That could be inner guidance, or it might be the small voice of Steven Bisyak, standing behind you, whispering in your ear!

Get quiet! Go within yourself. The little voice inside your head might also tell you, "Don't go." If that happens, you can ask for help. We have several firewalking instructors here tonight who can help you with the process and help you get past any problems that keep you from walking on the fire. Sometimes inner guidance will tell you not to walk on the fire. That's perfectly okay. Walking or not walking is not the point. The whole point of firewalking is *paying attention to and honoring your inner guidance*. There'll always be another fire. The important thing is not whether you walk or don't walk on fire tonight. The most important lesson you will learn here tonight is to follow your inner guidance and always walk the fire safely.

Your firewalk experience is a success whether you walk on fire or not, as long as you pay attention to your own inner guidance.

If your inner guidance tells you not to walk, don't walk. If you violate inner guidance and walk anyway, there is a strong likelihood you'll get burned.

If you don't hear a voice inside your head (not everyone does) telling you to walk or not to walk, there's another way to get a reading on inner guidance. Pay attention to your body because your body will never lie to you. You may find yourself standing in front of the fire pushing up and down on your toes. Maybe you'll be teetering toward the fire and nearly falling on your face. That's another way of getting in touch with inner guidance. Your body is full of energy, primed and pumped, ready to go. Yet you're standing there, paralyzed and terrified, with your feet riveted to the ground. Your legs are shaking and your body is leaning forward. That's when you should just let go and walk. When you're in that high energy state, chances are excellent you won't get burned. Simply let go, walk, and you'll be fine. Inner guidance will never let you down.

Pay attention to inner guidance. It's not going to yell at you, "GO!!!" "WALK ON THE FIRE!!!!!!!!!" It's going to be very quiet and still, so you'll need to really LISTEN or you won't hear it. You have to pay 100% attention. What's the worst thing you can think of that could happen to you if you walked on fire tonight?

Bill   I could burn my feet!

Diane   Not being able to walk.

Lois   A person could actually die . . . I read where that has happened at some firewalks in other countries. . . .

Terry   Maybe not die, but end up with a nasty burn!

Heather   The worst thing that could happen to me tonight is to come to this workshop, get offered this fabulous opportunity, and not use it. Not walking is the worst thing that could possibly happen to me here tonight! It would be better for me to walk and burn myself than to let this golden opportunity pass me by!

Mark   Harborview burn ward, here I come!! I might end up in a wheelchair.

Jason   Plastic feet!

Ted   Falling face down into the fire!

Steven   Falling into the fire . . . uh, huh!! That's probably the worst thing I could imagine. (Steven takes two steps forward in front of the class and falls flat on the floor on his hands with a CRASH! to dramatize this point.)

Falling Into the Fire

It actually happened at Harbin Hot Springs, California, at one of my seminars! The fire pit was surrounded by huge boulders, so you couldn't escape by jumping to the side of the fire. An elderly man, about 70 years old, wearing a full-body cast, came to the seminar with the intention of learning how to use his mind to heal his body.

He shuffled into the coal bed and tripped over a rock. We all watched in horror as he dove face first into the blazing coal bed. I could swear to this day I watched his foot melt completely off. Here this guy was, laying face down in the coal bed. I had to do something, *fast*, to save this guy's life! I'd already walked across that inferno once that night and was not about to do it again! That fire was *extremely HOT*. You could have waved a $1000 bill in my face and I wouldn't have sprinted across that fire again. But here we had a man lying face down in a red hot fire!! Somebody had to save him. I ran toward the heatwave of that inferno to try to save that senior citizen's life, but he got back up on his feet!! Amazingly, he actually started walking backwards out of the fire! We found out later, he remembered the workshop taught him that once you take a step into the fire, you walk the distance. There's no jumping out halfway through. So he reversed directions and proceeded to walk all the way through the coal bed. He didn't even get a blister!! Not a hair on his body was burned! Not a blister, not a mark! Out of the 70 people who walked that night, he was the only one who had no blisters, no symptoms, no marks. He said he felt no heat in the fire. Strange things have happened at firewalks—amazing things. If the worst happened to you tonight, could you accept it? Can you accept the possibility of getting burned tonight?

Mark   You'd have to.

Steven   Right, Mark. You have to be willing to accept the risk. If you can't accept the risk, you have no business walking on fire. A while ago, I asked how many long-term veteran firewalkers had been burned, and you saw how many people raised their hands. One hundred percent!

Jason   If you get a really bad burn, you might have to crawl on your hands and knees to the bathroom. The pain could be excruciating.

Terry   I've crawled to bed in agony several times asking myself, "Why did I have to do this to myself?"

Susan   What is the state of mind, the mental attitude, that causes someone to get burned?

Steven   I can think of several examples from my own personal experience. They were the most beneficial walks I ever experienced. I say that because I learned the most in firewalking and in life from my failures. I have used my failures as stepping stones on the road to success. One instance was in 1986 in Wenatchee. I received the worst burn I ever got in a fire. We were walking in front of TV cameras for a local news program. On my eighth trip across the fire, I glanced over at the TV cameras, wondering what I looked like on the camera (ego). It was like putting my foot in a tiger's mouth! I got such a bad burn on one foot, I had to crawl to the bathroom for seven days. It was 30 days before I could put my shoe back on!

123

Ego Makes the Fire Burn

Joe Toast

I *wasn't paying attention* to what I was doing. I was in my ego! Fire is real, regardless of what size it is! A tiny cigarette can put you in the hospital. So can a single match! I thought that because I had walked on the fire successfully seven times, the fire couldn't burn me on the eighth time! I learned a painful lesson that night. That lesson will stay with me for the rest of my life. There's no use dwelling on horror thoughts. Once you've taken a look at the worst that can possibly happen, let those horror thoughts go. It's history. After all, the worst that you can imagine is only a thought anyway, and it's a pretty negative thought, isn't it? So let that go, and then ask yourself, "What is the best that could possibly happen if I walk on fire?" Expecting the best in any given situation always attracts positive results.

Susan   I could be successful at this and not burn myself.

Jeff   The best thing that could possibly happen would be to overcome my fear of firewalking and then use the principles that I learn from firewalking to achieve success in all areas of my life.

George   I might walk into the fire and experience no heat on my feet.

Mary   I could get the self-confidence I've been seeking in all areas of my life.

Heather   Maybe I'll be able to remove some of the blocks in my life and thereby accomplish my dreams.

Steven   You can apply the techniques you're learning tonight to all areas of your life. These principles directly apply to all things you want to achieve. When most people experience fear, they want to get out of the situation as soon as possible. You hear them say things like, "I don't want to figure it out. Man, I don't want anything to do with it. Get me outta here!" Before I firewalked, that's exactly how I felt. I wasn't aware of how I habitually reacted to fear. Not until I walked on fire. I walked toward that first fire and hit what I call a *membrane of fear* about four feet from the edge of the coal bed. Man, it was heavy, like a solid wall. I became acutely aware in that instant that fear had been ruling my life. It was a very familiar and disturbing emotion. I would never allow myself to experience it for very long. I certainly never got to know fear intimately. Fear felt so uncomfortable to me that I actually ran away from it.

A POSITIVE ATTITUDE ATTRACTS POSITIVE RESULTS

125

After walking on fire, however, I no longer felt it was necessary to run from fear. After I walked on fire, when I felt fear, I would say, "Oh, that's just fear. It's so familiar." Until that shift in my conscious awareness, fear prevented me from doing what I wanted to do in life. Now I had options. I was no longer blocked and limited by fear. I had choices. I was no longer obligated to react and run from fear. Feeling fear became okay. Fear became acceptable to me. Now I could feel tremendous fear and *walk right through it*. It was just like a magic trick. False Evidence Appearing Real. The instant I walked through my fear, it disappeared. It ceased to exist. That's because the only fear that exists is in the mind, and it's all a production of the mind—it's entirely self-created.

Once you walk on fire, you can walk through False Evidence Appearing Real, and you will be able to do anything you want to do in life.

Firewalking Removes Self-Imposed Limitations

Think about your life. Decide which things are the most important to you. Put your priorities in order. Do the things you want to do. Begin *NOW*. Not tomorrow, not next month, not next year.

Tomorrow never comes. Today is all there is. Famous Amos says,

Today is worth two tomorrows.

If you want to grow, do things that will help you change and grow. Make a mental plan. Decide how you are going to get to your goal. If you want to take a trip, the first thing you have to do is to locate your destination on a map. Is there any way you're going to get to your destination if you don't know where you're going?

Imagine yourself walking up to a travel agent and saying, "I want to take a trip."

The agent asks you, "Where do you want to go?"

You reply, "I don't know exactly. I'm not sure."

The agent says, "We have airplanes that can take you anywhere you want to go in the world. Unless you decide where you're going, I can't give you a ticket."

Here's another illustration. From now on begin to think of yourself in a place we'll call *POINT A*. Point A is where you are right now. *POINT B* is anywhere you want to go. Point B is always your end goal. When you reach point B, it becomes point A. From now on, think of achieving goals as going from point A to point B.

	This analogy directly relates to firewalking. Firewalking is done by walking out of point A toward point B. Where is point A when you firewalk?
Jeff	Point A is right where you are when you're standing in front of the coal bed.
Steven	That's right. Where's point B?
Jeff	Point B is your goal, your destination, where you want to end up. We define that as three feet beyond the end of the coal bed.
Steven	Right again, Jeff. Focus on point B. There's a reason for point B being *three feet beyond the end of the coal bed.* Whether you walk on a 12-foot, a 20-foot, or a 120-foot-long fire, you'll find when you get down to the last two or three steps that you'll tend to lose your focus. You'll get down to the last two or three steps on the fire and you'll think, "I made it!!" Then you'll stop paying attention. Suddenly, "YAH WHOO-OOOOO!!!!! OOUUUUCHHHHHH!!!!" *You didn't make it!* You didn't go the distance. You weren't off the coal bed. I've been there. That's why I say, don't lose your focus, don't relax until after you've completely achieved your goal. Pay 100% attention until you're completely off the coal bed. Most people give up just before they achieve success. They *almost* make it. With another 10% effort, they would have done it.

It seems to be a law or a principle that distractions come your way to test your commitment, just before you succeed at anything in life. If you're not totally committed, that's where you "lose it."

Terry   I was laid up in bed with burned feet for a month. I was three feet from the end of the coal bed. I thought it was all over, thought I had it made, when suddenly—POW!!! Blister city!! I'm a slow learner.

Heather   How did Geraldo Rivera do with the firewalk?

Steven   He cooked. After the show, we went back to his dressing room and we counted 20 marks on one foot, 15 on the other. He was sitting on his counter with his feet in a sink full of ice water. The day before, Tolly Burkan tried to explain to him about burns. Geraldo's response was, "*Nobody burns Geraldo.*" Because of his overconfidence, Geraldo set up his own burn previous to the show.

After Geraldo blistered himself, Tolly and I explained a healing technique to him called Jin-Shin-Jitsu. When we were sure he had it down, we left Geraldo, who was practicing it. The next morning, Gerald called us on the phone. He was very ecstatic because when he awoke that morning, his blisters had entirely vanished. He said, "My blisters are completely gone!! I can't believe this! I'm stunned. You can quote me!!" Geraldo was ecstatic at this overnight healing of his feet.

Terry   That's true. Nobody burns you. You burn you.

Steven   Napoleon Hill wrote in *Think and Grow Rich*, "Whatever your mind can conceive and believe you can achieve." Never forget that. Everything begins with an attitude or a thought. Before we achieved the *Guinness Book of World Records* Hottest Firewalk, it was only a thought, just an idea. When we torched off that world record hottest fire, it looked like it was humanly impossible to cross it with bare feet. I had walked on fire 600 times previous to that world record walk. It looked absolutely impossible to me. The coal bed was deep! It was white hot, with flames three inches high dancing on top of the coals. We had industrial fans blasting air through it to make it hotter than a forge. The fans melted down.

The firepit was long. The court reporter told me, "If you screw up on this fire, you're going to end up with plastic feet in the Harborview burn ward. If you manage to survive, you'll never get out of your wheelchair! This is INSANE!!! *You can't do this!* IMPOSSIBLE, IMPOSSIBLE, IMMMMPPPPOOOOOSSIBLE!!!" Scientists from the University of Washington verified the temperature for us. "The temperature is climbing again," they said. "1445°, 1450°, 1475°." We had to get above 1494°, the previous world's record.

"1503°!" the scientist shouted. "You are now above the previous world's record. If you're going to do it, do it now!" I took one last look at all the horror thoughts I had in my head and let them go. I brought *Guinness Book of World Records* into my mind until it filled my consciousness completely. I paid 100% attention to that high thought. Nothing else existed. That's the only thing that I filled my mind with. When I walked across that fire, it was absolutely cool. Not a hair on my body was singed. I had made a mental plan, followed through with my plan, and it worked!

When you feel in your mind it's the right time for you to walk, then go. Take action. People sometimes call this "gut feeling." I like to call it inner guidance. Knowledge is useless unless it's applied. Take action. Follow your plan. Once you've made your mental plan, commit yourself to it. Then take action and follow through.

Jason   Don't let fear limit you now.

Steven   Let's go! Breaking bricks helps you get across that fire safely. It builds your energy.

5% Talk—95% Action!

[At this point in the seminar, the class begins to get up and exit the building. Outside, Douglas firs tower over 100 feet in the air, as if overseeing all the activity with detached observation. The moon is just breaking through the peaks of firs, bringing a lightness that reveals snow-capped mountains across the valley. One by one, each student is handed a brick, and then each student breaks a brick with his or her hand in front of the class. There is a great deal of excitement. Applause, ecstatic screams of joy, and excitement ripple through the class like an electric current as one by one all the bricks are smashed with resounding cracks and thuds as they fall heavily, pulverized on the brickstand, wasted and demolished. After the bricks are broken, the class continues, walking up the hill to the pulley swing, and later, convenes around the crackling fire.]

Steven   Susan, how do you feel after breaking your brick?

Susan   Awesome, excellent. Alive, very much so. When I was standing there just before I broke the brick, my heart was racing a mile a minute. It was fantastic; euphoria!! I can't believe I did it! I can't wait to show my daughter my broken brick!!

Steven   George, how did you feel about breaking your brick?

George   I felt amazed and I felt wonderful. My hand slid through that brick just like a knife through butter! I had a very strong visualization of the brick cracking before I actually hit it!

Steven   Another thing to keep in mind is the infinite difference between trying something and doing something. "T-R-Y" is the terrible "T" word. Look at this lighter in my hand. "Try" to take this lighter out of my hand. Don't actually do it, just try. Here you go, Mary, try to take the lighter out of my hand. What happens?

Mary   I'm holding back a little bit from actually doing it.

Steven   Were you successful?

Mary   No.

Steven   Why couldn't you do it?

Mary   Because I held back. I was only trying; I wasn't actually doing it.

Steven   That's right. There's no way you can "try" to walk on fire. You either do it or you don't. There's no way to "try" to break bricks. If you actually *DO IT*, your hand might sting a little bit for a couple of minutes. But if all you do is "*TRY*," the brick gets thick and hard and you end up with a mighty sore hand. There's no way to go down a pulley swing, jump out of an airplane, jump off a bridge, ask for a job, ask for a raise, or confront a problem in a relationship if all you do is just "try."

My personal motto is "5% talk, 95% action." The word "try" immediately sets you up for failure. It lets you off the hook and gives you excuses. It gives you the excuse to say, "*Well, I tried that.*" Erase the word "try" from your vocabulary!

Jeff   You're in control of your life. There's nobody out there to tell you that you can go for it. You have to want to. You have to decide to do it, not just to try.

Steven   There's no such word for us. Whatever we focus our attention on, we're going to get. Suddenly we're 100% responsible for the results we're getting in life. Do we want it? When we focus on the wrong thing, we get it. Then, oftentimes we cry out, "*I DON'T WANT IT!!!!!*"

Jeff   You have to be more clear on what you really want. You're in charge. Your mind creates your reality.

Susan   After we cross the fire, what happens if a little coal gets stuck between your toes?

Steven   That's called a cling-on. The best thing to do for a cling-on is to kick your foot real hard and the cling-on should fly off—or just reach down with your hand and wipe it off. The grass is usually pretty wet this time of year. When your feet are wet, you tend to get more cling-ons.

Great! Let's all go gather around the firepit now for some final preparation.

[The firepit is 12 to 14 feet long and about four feet wide, set in the middle of an emerald green lawn. There are some lawn chairs set about so that people can sit and observe, or easily remove their shoes when the coals are raked out and it's time for the actual firewalk. The air is clean and crisp, and the scent of evergreen wafts into the air. The atmosphere becomes light around the fire, as if everyone were having an experience around a campfire.]

Steven   We do our best to keep the mouth of the fire pit clear so that people who are walking toward the fire don't get blocked by other people standing in the way. We'll form two lines. Nobody should be standing in the center or blocking the way to the fire pit unless you're ready to go.

Again, what is your intention? It should be to get across the fire pit safely. Make your intention clear. Safety first. Don't dip your toe in the coals to find out if they're hot!

Remember that burns tend to occur when people aren't paying attention. The mind gets distracted or the ego gets involved.

Leonard   Ego is the worst.

Terry   Ego is the thing that's the most deceptive. I've walked on fires that were perfect. Cold fires. Then, suddenly, this little bitty puppy bites me!! Two steps were cool, but that next step, man, it was HOT!

The thermostat jumped from zero degrees to 1200° in a millisecond. Time magically froze. It all happened quicker than you can snap your fingers. I lost my focus and fried my foot.

Steven   Reality kicks in. The fire can bite you if you're not paying attention. It's important for you to prepare mentally. We call that "logging it in." It's like programming your mind, just the same as you'd program a computer. You mentally prepare for what's about to happen.

Terry   If you ask any of the experienced firewalkers here tonight if they're experiencing fear, the answer is going to be a resounding "yes."

Jeff   I don't want to get rid of my fear completely. Fear is healthy.

Steven   I'd like to share something with those of you who are here tonight for your first firewalk. This first firewalk for you is a unique and special experience. There will never be another quite like it for you.

Tonight is a very magical night if it's your first time walking on fire. Now, it's time for a fireside story.

The Story of the Black Door

An Arab chief tells the story of a Persian general who had fallen upon a strange and weird custom. Any time a spy was captured, he was sentenced to death by the Persian general. He was always given a choice. He could either face the firing squad or he could pass through the black door.

As the moment of execution drew near, the general ordered the spy to be brought before him. The primary purpose was to find out which way this man wanted to die. Which shall it be? The firing squad or the black door?

This was not an easy question. The prisoner hesitated, but he soon made it known that he much preferred the firing squad. Not long thereafter, a volley of shots announced that the grim sentence had been fulfilled. The general turned to his aides and said, "You see how it is with men? They will always choose the known way to the unknown. It is a characteristic of people to be afraid of the undefined. Yet, I have given him a choice."

"What lies behind the black door?" asked the aide.

"Freedom," replied the general. "I have known only a few men brave enough to claim it."

Steven   *Tonight's your black door!*

[As people are walking on the fire, Steven works with some first-time firewalkers who are hesitating.]

[Whispering]   Picture what you want on the other side of the fire. Go for it! Let your horror thoughts go! Focus on the best that can happen! Follow your plan, then go for it. Take action!

[After all the first-time firewalkers have gone across the fire, the group is aglow with the excitement of achievement. The last call is given for walking on the fire. When everyone is finished firewalking, the group walks down the wooded hill on the trail and reconvenes in the seminar building.]

I WALK ON FIRE
I CAN DO ANYTHING I CHOOSE

Steven   What we're talking about here is anything that's physically possible for you to do. Anything that anyone else can do, you can do. I'm not talking about going up on the 51st floor of the Columbia Center and then jumping out because you think you can now levitate. I'm talking about starting a business, asking for a raise, improving your relationship, or achieving anything in your life—putting your dreams into high gear. Fear can no longer limit you from achieving your hopes, goals, and dreams in life.

Fear can no longer hold you back and limit you in life because you now know how to take action in spite of fear.

Deciding what you want will probably be the most difficult thing for most of you. Once you use fear as a positive force in your life, all you have to do is decide what you want. Be clear in your intentions. Go ahead and feel the fear and then move through it just like you did when you walked on fire. Take action.

Does anybody want to share their experience?

Joe   I can still feel it in my hands and my feet. It feels like a numbness. It was like I went numb from the knees down. Then it clicked that I felt no pain when I walked on the fire. The feeling is starting to come back now, but there was a definite numbness . . .

Steve   With a tingling sensation?

Joe   Yes, a tingling. It really felt like an altered energy flow in my body. I felt a great deal of energy flowing through my hands.

Steven   What you're describing is a common sensation. It happens a lot among firewalkers. So, are you ready now to walk on your hands in the fire?

Joe   I may do a handstand in the gymnasium, but definitely not in the fire!

Steven   When you go to bed tonight, you'll probably be thinking, "Okay, I'm going to sleep now." You'll start drifting off to sleep and suddenly . . . *BAM!!* Your eyes will pop wide open.

139

That's a common experience for first-time firewalkers. That's what we call the firewalkin' blues. When you finally do fall asleep, you'll wake up in the morning and the first thought that will come to your mind is, "WHAT DID I DO LAST NIGHT??!!!"

Jason   Someone gave me a business card that said "Firewalking" on it. I got tremendously excited because I really wanted to firewalk. As soon as I made the call to enroll in the seminar, I was scared. I was literally gripped with the emotion of fear, thinking all the while, "Oh, my God, what have I done?"

I was scared out of my mind for three weeks. Bruce drove me up here. He said, "Okay, here we go!" I sat in the car for 15 minutes; I couldn't move because of fear. It was mighty intense. I wanted to puke.

Joe   When my foot first hit the fire, I could tell it was hot. My second step, I felt that it had to be cool. It turned ice cold; it felt like ice cubes. I'm ready to come back again!

Steven   Great! The fire is the greatest teacher I know. It gives you instantaneous feedback. I thank you all for being here tonight.

THE STEPS OF THE FIREWALKING SEMINAR

1. BE CLEAR IN YOUR INTENTION

2. PAY ATTENTION 100%

3. ASK YOURSELF: WHAT IS THE WORST THAT COULD POSSIBLY HAPPEN?
    If the worst happened, are you willing to accept it?
    If you're willing to accept the risk of the worst happening, then let your horror thoughts go.

4. ASK YOURSELF: WHAT IS THE BEST THAT COULD POSSIBLY HAPPEN?
    Focus on the best that could possibly happen. Hold those high thoughts in your mind.

5. DECIDE WHAT YOU WANT
    Make a 100% commitment.

6. MAKE A MENTAL PLAN
    Decide how you're going to get there.

7. GO—TAKE ACTION AND GIVE IT ALL YOU'VE GOT!!!

I think I can! I think I can!!
I THINK I CAN!!!

Lil' Toot

16

FOCUS ON THE BEST

A positive focus in your life can take many forms. For instance:

> personal growth
> success
> high self-esteem
> enjoying life
> loving yourself and others more
> making more money
> getting all you want out of life

The quality of your experience in life is the direct result of where your focus is. When you focus only on "what if's" and negative pictures of disasters in your future, it destroys your enjoyment of the moment. Letting go of fear means empowering yourself to have more fun in life. When you focus on the best, it allows you to take action. Fear cannot limit you.

If all you can think of is "What would my mother say?" shift your focus. If you can't think of one positive thing to focus on, find something in your field of vision and focus your mind on that. For instance, it could be a person, a tree, or a rock. It doesn't matter.

The point is, if you're paying 100% attention, you're only capable of focusing your mind on one thing at a time. If you focus on something other than your fear or negativity, that fear ceases to exist for you the moment you shift your focus.

Unless something is in your mind, it doesn't exist for you in that moment. It can't be a part of your reality unless you consciously perceive it or call it to mind by remembering it.

Pay attention
To what you see
For what you perceive is your
Reality

Michael McDermott

A monk was walking on a path in a jungle. Pretty soon a tiger started chasing him. The faster he ran, the faster the tiger ran. Soon the tiger joined two other tigers, who entered the chase. The monk ran over to the edge of a cliff and grabbed on to a vine. As he hung on to the vine, he saw below him three tigers waiting for him to fall. Just then, a rat came to the edge of the cliff and began chewing through the vine that the monk was holding on to.

In that moment, the monk glanced up and saw a small strawberry. Just before he fell from the cliff, he popped the strawberry into his mouth. He enjoyed that strawberry so much that he didn't even mind falling off the cliff and being eaten by the tigers!

The moral of the story is: The monk had practiced meditation all his life. Because of this, he had the ability to pay 100% attention. By paying 100% attention to the experience of the strawberry in his mouth, everything else ceased to exist for him in that moment. When he popped the strawberry into his mouth, the tigers disappeared, and the fear vanished. He became one with the experience of eating the strawberry and everything else, in his perception, ceased to exist.

Focus is determination. When you break a brick, you realize it's possible that you could pulverize your hand. So you accept that possibility. Then you focus your mind on the best. You visualize the brick breaking in half, and you see your hand going completely through it. You determine the outcome by your focus. Believe in yourself 100%. You have to be 100% committed and you can't just try. Nobody ever did anything by "trying." There's a world of difference between trying and doing.

Focus is like a laser beam. When light is diffused, it has little power; it's very weak, like a fluorescent light. Focus those same light rays into a laser beam, and you can cut through the toughest diamond with that focused light! A laser beam is focused, and it can penetrate anything because the rays are focused. Your mind is like that. Intelligence, power, and ability are direct results of mental focus or concentration.

Concentration, focusing your mind and believing in yourself 100%, is the key to success, whether you're breaking a brick or meeting a challenge on the job. Put emotion behind your focus. Bending rebar takes that kind of focus. When you're standing with the sharp end of a rebar against your throat, you realize it could puncture your throat. It could puncture your windpipe and lacerate your spine. You could get a tracheotomy! It can be very scary.

Focusing is like flipping a switch in your mind. You focus on the center of the bar, think "bend," and go for it. You have to give it 100% commitment or it *just will not happen*.

Focusing on the best helps you tremendously! It will give you the ability to accomplish whatever you want to in life! You can have successful relationships, make more money, and achieve success. Spend some time each day focusing on positive outcomes for all the problems that come up from time to time in your life. Focus on the best that can possibly happen and it probably will!

17

TAKE ACTION

*The ancestor of every action
is a thought*

Emerson

*Faced with crisis, people of action
fall back and rely upon themselves.
These people create results by taking action,
taking responsibility for results, and*
MAKING THINGS HAPPEN.
Difficulty attracts people of character
because it is by embracing difficulty and
taking *ACTION* in the moment that
YOU REALIZE WHO YOU ARE.

All achievement in life is based on a person being able to take action. Taking action means that you have to be able to recognize what your fear is. Then you need to MOVE through that fear, toward the object of your desire.

You can use that principle to ask for a raise in pay, to get a new job, to start a new relationship, to confront an unpleasant situation, or to take a walk on fire.

MOVE

and

TRUST

Trust is one of my favorite words. But you say, "How am I supposed to trust when I'm scared to death?" As with everything in your reality, in your life, trust is a state of mind. When you want to take action, trust is what you want to focus on. Some people trust God; some people trust themselves. Some people don't trust anyone or anything, including themselves. Whatever you choose to trust is up to you. It can be God, spirit, higher self, Jesus, The Force, mother nature, Mohammed, the energy, the odds, Krishna, your mother, the almighty dollar, Buddha, or simply yourself. Trust relates to faith, and faith is power. Conceive your own power base. It can be whatever you really believe in. The following story gives an illustration of how trust works.

A man and his wife were driving home one night. As the car turned the corner into their neighborhood, they noticed a blaze of fire and smoke coming from their house.

The babysitter was in the front yard with two of the children who had escaped from the burning house.

A five-year old child, Christopher, was trapped on the third floor of the house, which was rapidly being engulfed by flames and about to explode.

"Christopher! JUMP!!! JUMP!!!" the father screamed.

"Papa! Papa!" the boy yelled frantically. "I can't see you!"

"I know," the father yelled back. "*But I can see you!*" Instantly Christopher jumped into his father's arms and was safe.

Taking action means moving from the known into the unknown. When Christopher jumped out of the window, he couldn't see his father. He had to move and trust, knowing that he would be okay, trusting his father to catch him. He had to have faith. Taking action, moving and trusting, fear is overcome, mastered, and vanquished!

Knowledge is useless without action

Steven Bisyak

It's important to take action *NOW* because there are no guarantees on the future. I keep reminding people, "Okay, let's be in the moment. Do what you want to do. *Take action in spite of your fear. Don't let fear limit you. Don't let fear hold you back.*" I don't want to be lying on my deathbed saying, "I wish I had done this; if only I had done that; if only, if only, if only, ..."

Since learning to firewalk, I take action and accomplish whatever I really want to do in this life. My desire is to pass these keys along to as many people as I can.

"Try" is the "Terrible T Word"
Don't just try
Take action and do it!

All NEGATIVE action in life is based in fear
All POSITIVE action in life is based in love

Steven Bisyak

18

HEALING STATES OF MIND AND BODY PIERCING

To the casual observer, it looks freaky to watch someone run a five-inch doll needle through his hand. It seems bizarre, even crazy.

Body piercing, to me, is a deliberate exercise in controlling pain that gets spontaneous results.

If you put a needle against your skin and then apply pressure, most people will stop doing it once they begin to feel pain and discomfort. However, if you do it as a challenge, pain is the point at which you become very serious about your mental focus. Also, if your intention is to do it without pain and without blood, that's the result you'll achieve. Piercing your hand with a needle is somewhat of an illusion. The reason for this is that to the observer it appears excruciating. For the person doing the piercing, however, the most pain is actually felt where the needle pierces the skin on the top and where it comes out the other side in the palm of the hand. Usually you don't hit any nerves in the muscle.

The skin layer is the toughest part to pierce, so the needle goes through the muscle like a knife through butter and there is little, if any, pain.

Psychologists have discovered that most people only use about ten to 12% of their mental capacities or brain power. What would happen if we put the other 88 to 90% to use?

One way of dealing with pain is to go into it. You can either go into it, go out of it, or just accept it and let it be. Fighting the pain seems to be futile. Going into it, focus your mind 100% on the pain, feel the totality of it, experience the sensation 100%. Going out of it, concentrate the mind on something—anything other than the pain. It's also possible to feel the pain and just accept it. Usually the pain will lessen that way.

Another way of dealing with pain is to take on the pain of someone else you know who's hurting. Then take the pain of the world and add it to the rest of your pain. Just go ahead and feel it, completely and fully. Allow yourself to feel that it's okay that the pain is there (acceptance). Use the pain as energy to accomplish something, or let all that pain flow through you.

How do you psych yourself up to run a needle through your hand? One way is to believe that it's going to do something extremely positive for you. Otherwise, you probably won't do it. You should have a 100% commitment or it will be very difficult for you to get past the first layer of skin.

If you've never run a needle through your hand, how are you ever going to know what you'll feel like after you've done it, or what a positive difference it can make in your life?

"The proof of the pudding is in the eating." You can visualize yourself doing something, but it's never the same as the actual reality. You have to take action to get results. Action produces results.

There is no substitute for action

One technique of mind control that can help with body piercing is one that has been used by Hindu Yogis for thousands of years. Imagine that your hand and your arm are pieces of wood. It may be difficult to run a needle through your own flesh unless you're somehow able to change your state of mind.

Another way is to visualize the atoms and molecules of your hand separating and opening in order to make room for the needle as you visualize the point of the needle sliding through the flesh.

I've discovered by experience that the needle can focus and amplify energies in the body. Undoubtedly, this is what Chinese doctors discovered thousands of years ago when they discovered *Ki* (life force or life energy). The energies inspired them to create the incredible system of Chinese acupuncture.

When you practice firewalking, bungee jumping, sky diving, rappeling, and body piercing, you discover that once you've made a commitment, saying, "Okay, I'm going to do this," it's almost as if another force takes over, helping you take action to achieve your dream.

A particularly difficult type of pain to deal with is emotional pain. When we feel the pain of a lost love or a broken relationship, that pain is entirely created and recreated by *our own thought* through the power of memory. If we had no memory, it would be impossible to put ourselves through emotional pain again and again, experiencing sorrow and grief over loss.

One way to get out of emotional pain is to focus strongly on the present—on the activity you are doing in the moment. Emotional pain will cease to exist for you the moment you choose to pay 100% attention to something else.

In his book *Love, Medicine and Miracles*, Dr. Bernie Siegel says that the best patients are the "worst," the most difficult. They argue with the doctor. They don't just accept the diagnosis, saying, "Doctor, I agree with you," and roll over and die. They have a fighting spirit. They have a tremendous will to live. They take a look at themselves and get in touch with their feelings.

They recognize the areas in their lives where they've been denying themselves and they commit themselves to making positive changes in their lives. If the mind can make you sick, the mind can make you well.

There have been several cases of healing among firewalkers. One of these cases concerns a man who is over the age of 50. He was diagnosed with colon cancer four times. Every time he went in for his diagnosis, he ended up "telling off" the doctors. "I don't buy that," he said. "I refuse to accept your diagnosis. I don't believe it. Because I don't believe it, it's not true for me."

On his fifth and final diagnosis, the day before the scheduled operation to remove the cancer, the doctors discovered the cancer was gone. Somehow, the cancer mysteriously vanished. Where did it go? This is a documented medical case. This same man decided he was going to get into a healthy condition. He trained and ran in a marathon and took first place ahead of 2000 competitors in his age range—well over 50 years old! He has a new wife, a new house, and he is now living his life to the max!

Another man had a disintegrated hip. Before he went into surgery, he consulted with his doctor. "It'll take you about a month before you're well enough to go home," the doctor advised him.

"Doctor," he said, "you don't understand. *I'm a firewalker. I don't buy that. I don't put any such limitations on myself.*" After the operation, the staff was astonished when he left the hospital in three days. Follow-up x-rays revealed that this man's bones were actually growing to replace what he lost. Medical science says that isn't supposed to happen. Science says it's impossible.

Once you accept 100% responsibility for yourself, you have claimed your power. We've been giving our power away all our lives and accepting artificial limitations. We give our power away all the time to doctors, politicians, lawyers, family members—almost anybody and everybody.

Some people come to a firewalk and have their money issues addressed. Then they can really begin to address those issues and change their beliefs around the issue of money.

Several people who believed lack of money was limiting them from buying a house purchased a house within one week after firewalking. They definitely experienced a financial healing.

One man was in his seventies. "The bank doesn't want to lend me any money," he told us at the workshop. "Who wants to lend money to a man who's going to be over 100 years old by the time he pays it back?" After the firewalk, this same elderly gentleman was ecstatic. His spirit was on fire. Within three days, he purchased a beautiful home on two acres of land in one of the most beautiful places in the Northwest. He credits the change in his attitude and getting his house to the firewalk experience.

This same man had a case of athlete's foot for over 20 years. After walking on fire, the athlete's foot cleared up and has never returned. The fungus apparently said, "I'm out of here!"

The mind has a powerful effect on the body. About a week after one lady walked on fire, the people at her office told her, "That's impossible. You can't do that! You didn't do it. If you had walked on fire, you would have been burned."

After a time, she began to believe it. One morning about a week *after the firewalk* she woke up with blisters on her feet. Because of that experience, she learned not to buy into other people's beliefs as much any more.

Another example is when that same lady broke both of her ankles. She got frustrated and angry. She said, "My kids need me. This should never have happened to me! Those kids need me and *I will heal! I need to be well right away!*"

In two days she was walking on two shattered ankles that healed almost overnight. That's a poignant example of how the mind can be used to heal the body. It begins with intent. If your mind is made up 100%, it helps your body heal.

Three scientists attended a firewalking workshop and nobody in attendance got burned. They went back to the laboratory later that week to "dissect" the firewalk experience, and all of those scientists got burned. The way you think about the experience determines the outcome. Think negative about it and you get negative results. Think positive about it and let it be a *positive* experience.

"Sometimes a hobby can end up being worth millions."

Steven Bisyak

19

CHALLENGES UNLIMITED, INC.

When Challenges Unlimited, Inc., ("CU") was created by Steven Bisyak in 1984, the intention was and continues to be to create a supportive environment for people who want to master their fears. CU offers a wide variety of activities and adventures that help people to do just that. The emphasis is definitely on taking action, even when the mind, body, and emotions are set against it because of the emotion of fear. The purpose of CU is to provide mutual support and encouragement to help people move beyond self-limitation in a variety of situations. The emphasis is on changing states of mind and perceptions. The motto of CU is "5% talk, 95% action."

CU is a serious, committed core group of individuals dedicated to self-mastery and unlimitedness. CU seeks out and finds ways in which each person can experience fully what he or she desires to experience in the way of personal challenge. The format provides ongoing opportunities for self-advancement, personal achievement, and socializing fun.

CU is a group composed of "hard-core" firewalkers. Among those people who are hard cores, there's still a lot of work to be done because there are other specific fears that need to be confronted—for instance, fear of heights, or fear of spiders and snakes. Just because you've walked on fire once or even a number of times doesn't mean that you've completely mastered fear. It takes more than that. Walking on fire is a great way to start!

There's a big difference between the "casual" or one-time firewalker and "hard-core" firewalkers. I've seen thousands of people walk on fire. It's a mighty powerful experience. However, very few people keep coming back and continuing to firewalk on a long-term basis. For most people, it's a one-shot deal. It's a big deal, that's true. Ask anyone who walked on fire three or four years ago, just once, and they'll invariably tell you that it was a major turning point in their lives.

You begin to crack the "cosmic egg" (which is your own fear and self-limiting beliefs) the first time you walk on fire. As you continue confronting fear and walking on fire, the cracks in your own "cosmic egg" become bigger and bigger. When you've walked on fire hundreds of times, whole chunks start falling off the "cosmic egg," and you are free. You know the difference between illusion and reality. You see the universe for what it really is, and you know who you are. You no longer have to limit yourself.

Steven Bisyak & Michael McDermott

Guinness Book of World Records

On September 19, 1987, for the *Guinness Book of World Records*, a group of 11 people broke the world's record for the hottest fire ever walked on bare-foot by a human being. Most of the people at that event were members of CU. We had research scientists from the University of Washington monitoring the event. The coals were ten to 12 inches deep and 16 feet long, and flames were dancing three inches above the four-foot-wide coal bed. It looked absolutely impossible. I looked at it and thought, "What am I doing here? This is impossible. No one can walk on this one!" I accepted the possibility that I could end up in a wheelchair without feet. We had fans forcing air through the fire to make it heat like a forge; we melted the fans. People operating the fans got their faces and arms burned and blistered from the radiant heat alone. Some of those burns were fairly serious.

I was able successfully to face my fear and walk across that fire. I went first. We broke the old world record temperature by 52°. That doesn't seem like very much, but when you're talking about 1546°, that's an extremely hot fire to be walking on. Three weeks later, members of CU set up and walked the longest firewalk in the recorded history of the world. It was a 120-foot-long bed of blazing hot coals. Prior to our 120-foot firewalk, the record had been held by the University of Hawaii football team. They had done a firewalk of 60 feet. CU had already done four 50-foot firewalks. It had been a fabulous experience. The group thought that if a 50-foot walk was good, then a 120-foot firewalk would be even better.

We burned ten cords of wood, all in one long line, in order to make a 120-foot-long coal bed. Not everyone was able to walk the entire 120 feet. Some people were only able to walk 12 feet of the 120-foot coal bed. Others walked 110 feet and could not make the last ten feet. The state of mind you're in definitely has a bearing on your ability to walk on fire. If you're thinking negative, you get a negative result. If you think positive, you get a positive result. It has a lot to do with the energy that's in your body. Think about it. You can end up in the hospital by stepping on a lit cigarette with bare feet. How could you possibly walk across 120 feet of red hot coals without being burned? Yes, people can and do work miracles. Never underestimate the power of your mind.

20

THE DENIAL OF FEAR

*I discovered that there's only
one way to handle fear:
Go out and scare yourself!*

Do the thing you fear, then watch it disappear!

*Prior to the firewalk, I had no fear!
That's because I didn't do anything
that stimulated fear!*

Steven Bisyak

Recognizing that fear is a normal part of the human experience is a big step toward mastering fear. There is an almost overwhelming tendency to cover up and deny fear. This chapter identifies some common fears that are frequently overlooked or denied.

Mastering Fear: The Ultimate Challenge

According to statistics compiled by the National Highway Traffic Safety Administration, in 1990, 44,529 people were killed in fatal automobile crashes in the United States. Approximately half of those fatalities were alcohol-related. Fatalities per 100,000 licensed drivers were 26.66. Every year there are about 1,700,000 disabling automobile injuries. The death rate per 100 million vehicle miles for 1990 was 2.1 people.

Every day, on the average, 122 people in the U.S. are killed and 4722 people are disabled in automobile accidents! In spite of those grim statistics, people ride in automobiles every day; they don't stop driving. Driving an automobile is a very common and familiar thing to do. It's an acceptable risk, thought of as being necessary. It's done so many times and so often that people are not consciously aware of real dangers and the risks involved. If fear were a rational thing, getting into an automobile should be a very scary behavior, but it's not for most people, because they drive cars so often that they are desensitized to the risk.

Driving is a serious risk. Most people are nervous, scared, and even terrified the first time they drive a car. They realize how risky it is when they first start doing it.

The level of fear one experiences is not always based on the actual risk. Fear is not based on reason; it's an emotional reaction. The psychology of desensitization clearly demonstrates that the more one experiences any risky activity, the less fear one will have. Driving an automobile is risking injury or death, but it's not commonly perceived as being risky. Because driving is so familiar, it's a good example of desensitization.

Many people don't master fear because they don't know what their fear is. Some people seem to have a fear of their own fear. In order to fix a problem, or achieve a solution, one must first admit that there is a problem. Thus, the first step in mastering fear is to admit there is fear. In order to do that, one must know what fear is.

What is fear? Fear is observed in the following classical symptoms with which everyone is familiar. According to *Webster's Ninth New Collegiate Dictionary*:

> Fear is an emotional reaction, often violent, to a real or imagined threat. Fear in human beings is believed to be learned rather than instinctive. Shortly after birth, the young of many animals are capable of well-coordinated withdrawal or flight reactions when confronted with a frightening stimulus. The human infant, however, does not display any such coordinated fear response.

> Fear: an unpleasant often strong emotion caused by anticipation or awareness of danger; a state marked by this emotion; anxious concern; . . . reason for alarm. . . .

The emotion of fear isn't pleasant. It doesn't feel good. Fear produces guilty feelings, which usually result in a negative state of mind. For men, masculinity is at stake. For women, courage and fearlessness don't meld with society's stereotype for females.

Men grow up reading the John Wayne Handbook. The belief is that real men are tough and macho. They're fighters, not cowards. The bully is at the extreme end of the scale, however. The bully deals with fear by acting out aggression. That's a coverup for fear. Bullies are motivated by insecurity and fear.

> *I have no need to do that!*
> *Besides, the sky is falling!!!*

Chicken Little

Violent women are scary because they've stepped out of the expected code of behavior for females in our society. Bonnie and Clyde are an interesting example of the yin and yang of violence. Defiant, romantic violence is attractive. It's a distraction from one's own fears and violent tendencies. It's much easier for most people to see fear and violence in others than to recognize and admit it in themselves.

Fear is a powerful, unpleasant, and stressful emotion. Most people don't like to think about doing things that would allow them to feel fear.

When someone says, "I have no need to do that," they unconsciously limit themselves. The real reason such statements are made is because of some underlying fear. It's really a statement that there is "no need" to accept challenges that might cause personal growth and development. This is another way of saying there is "no need" for positive change. Behind this familiar cop-out is a fear of taking risks.

"Daredevils," on the other hand, are those weirdos who actually enjoy scaring themselves, their friends, and their mothers. If people enjoy things such as bungee jumping, skydiving, or motocross, they're sometimes put down. Some people defend themselves against involvement in the activities through putting them down. They resort to name calling, such as "adrenaline junkie" or "excitement addict." If the same people would let their hair down and let themselves go a little, they might experience a tremendous boost to their self-esteem without bodily injury. A major reason people develop fear is because they know little or nothing about a given activity. The common denominator is fear of the unknown. Bungee jumping, for instance, "appears" to be scary, so it's easy to react negatively to it. Once people participate in the experience, however, they are usually surprised by the great physical, emotional, and psychological benefits they get out of it. Some people hold back from bungee jumping and other challenging activities because of fear.

Construction workers can comfortably work hundreds of feet off the ground every day. People who have never worked under those conditions might become paralyzed by fear if they had to work that high up in the air.

Jane is an interesting lady. She's extremely frightened at the prospect of walking on fire. Yet, there she is, making six skydives every weekend from two miles high, freefalling for over 30 seconds per jump, with little or no fear.

Mastering Fear: The Ultimate Challenge

Perceptions of reality are colored and distorted by what is known and familiar. Because fear is an emotion that's not rational, people sometimes live with the illusion that they have "no fear." That's because they never allow themselves to do things that bring up fear. It's too uncomfortable to admit they're scared. Admitting fear, some people think, would be admitting weakness. After all, who wants to be called "chicken" or a "sissy"?

Fear can make one ill-at-ease, which is another way of saying fear is another disease. The key to understanding the disease of fear is understanding that fear is a disease of denial.

Denial and avoidance of fear is a cycle that increases with age. The older one becomes, the more likely he or she is to become conservative. After all, bones break, accidents happen, and day-to-day living is full of danger. As time goes by, most people are less and less inclined to take any risks with their physical bodies, their money, or even their time. Many people like to feel comfortable all the time. Fearing pain, people are afraid of the injuries that could cause pain.

Denying fear convinces people that they're not afraid. If they're questioned about the subject, they become defensive. Rather than taking risks and living life to the fullest, they get vicarious adventure by watching TV and videos. Safe in living rooms, detached from real life, a person doesn't actually have to come face to face with fear. Denial of fear becomes a constant state of mind. Horror stories such as those in Stephen King novels can become a masking over real fear inside an individual.

Daily newspapers are loaded with murder and mayhem. Violence and fear are the expected fare on the nightly news. Fear becomes "something out there."

When people habitually say "no" to experiences that could challenge them, expand their horizons, and bring enrichment to their lives, they're in denial of their fears. When fear buttons are pushed, instead of taking action, some people shut down.

When fear happens, physical, mental, and emotional changes take place. Adrenaline kicks in and an energy rush causes a person to sweat. People hyperventilate, throats tighten, there's cotton-mouth, stomachs knot up, and people get "butterflies."

Children feel this same energy and move naturally. It's all a part of child's play! They let it out and express it, moving, running, and jumping. A child's life is an adventure because children allow themselves to flow with the energy. Some adults feel the same energy and shut down. No wonder adult life can become boring, depressing, and uninteresting. It's created that way by attitudes and habits that result in positive or negative choices. Saying "yes" to energy, "yes" to movement, and "yes" to life is a conscious choice.

Say yes to life!!

Children jump up and down with excitement. Why don't most adults do that? Is it inhibition or fear of criticism? In reality, the physical symptoms of excitement and fear are identical. Naturally turning fear into excitement, children are teachers of the art of mastering fear.

Shutting down energy is shutting down life. Life is energy, movement, creation, and expression. Without risk, there's no movement, no life! No creation, no expression. *There's no life without risk!* Life is movement entwined with energy. When energy is spent, life force is renewed and it builds up the energy supply. As Paul Bragg, world-famous Ph.D. nutritionist and life-extension specialist, said:

It's better to wear out Than to rust out

Through unfortunate programming, and fear of rejection and disapproval, adults have a tendency to deny their feelings. Wanting acceptance, some people prefer to "be cool," instead of "letting their hair down" and just being themselves.

The table below lists a few of the excuses we commonly use to avoid challenging and enriching experiences.

Negative Response	*Positive Response*
I have no need to do that.	Because thousands of people are having a ball doing that, I might enjoy doing it, too!
I have no desire to do that.	That looks like a challenging activity. Let's go for it.

Negative Response	Positive Response
That's really, really stupid! It's dumb.	I'm not going to put a judgment on it until after I've done it. How can I know what the results are until after I've done it for myself?
I did it in my past life. I'll do it in my next life.	The past doesn't exist. The only time I have is *NOW*! I'm living my life in the present moment, not in the past or the future.
I might make a fool out of myself.	It wouldn't be the first time. Besides, the most important thing is the way I feel about myself, and not what others think of me.
I can't afford it.	That's baloney! I have enough money to do the things I really want to do in life. If I don't have the money, *I'll make the money!*
I have no time.	I always find time to do the things that make my life worthwhile and give me satisfaction and fulfillment.

Negative Response	Positive Response
I don't want to.	I'm not going to use this lame excuse any more. I choose to let go of ego, fear, and limitation and become who I truly am.
I'm afraid.	I admit the fear. It's okay; I don't deny it. I'll feel the fear and take action anyway. What have I got to lose?
I don't have a death wish!	That's a totally negative thought to what would probably be a very positive experience. Anyway, I might die tomorrow, so I should experience life today.

Think of a sentence that begins with the words, "*What if . . .*" *This always pinpoints the exact source of any fear.*

Think of the worst that could possibly happen. Could you accept it? The secret to taking action is to take a look at the horror thoughts in your mind and then let them go. Visualize the best that could possibly happen. Focus on the best of all possible outcomes. What if you break your leg getting out of bed? People have done it. Would you let that prevent you from ever getting up in the morning?

On the other hand, "what if" you get out of bed, go down to the 7-11, buy a lotto ticket, and WIN? That could happen, too. Let your horror thoughts go and focus on the best that could possibly happen. Let's take a look at a few "what if's" associated with some challenging activities:

What if the bungee cord breaks? (Fear of Injury or Death)

What if my mother finds out? (Fear of Mother)

What if I chicken out at the last minute? (Ego)

What if I can't do it? (Ego, Low Self-Esteem, Fear of Failure)

What if I'm injured and I can't work? (Economic Insecurity)

What if I get killed? (Fear of Death)

What if I skydive and the parachute doesn't open? (Fear of Heights, Fear of Dirt/Ground, Fear of Death)

What if I pay for a hang glide and then I chicken out? (Fear of Losing Money, Ego)

Fear is an extremely common human emotion. Psychology has put some pretty exotic names on some of our common fears. A phobia is defined as an abnormal, excessive dread or fear. Put a checkmark next to the fears you identify with — *pay attention!*:

acrophobia (heights) _____
agoraphobia (open spaces, market place, etc.) _____
ailurophobia (cats) _____
alchmophobia
(sharp objects) _____
algophobia (pain) _____
androphobia (men) _____
anthropophobia (people) _____
aquaphobia (water) _____
arachnophobia (spiders) _____
astraphobia (lightning) _____
aviaphobia (flying) _____
bacteriophobia (germs) _____
ballistophobia
(missiles) _____
baloneyphobia
(boring lectures, baloney sandwiches) _____
belonephobia
(needles, pins) _____
brontophobia (thunder) _____
claustrophobia
(closed spaces) _____
cynophobia (dogs) _____
dementophobia (madness) _____
dipsophobia (drink) _____
equinophobia (horses) _____
erythrophobia
(blushing) _____
genophobia (sex) _____
gymnophobia (nakedness) _____
hemophobia (blood) _____

herptophobia (snakes, lizards, and other crawling things)	_____
hypnophobia (falling asleep)	_____
lalophobia (talking)	_____
lyssophobia (becoming insane)	_____
melissophobia (bees)	_____
murophobia (mice)	_____
mysophobiagerms (dirt)	_____
nyctophobia (darkness)	_____
ochlophobia (crowds)	_____
osmophobia (odors)	_____
pedophobia (children)	_____
photophobia (light)	_____
pyrophobia (fire)	_____
siderodromophobia (railroads)	_____
sitophobia (eating)	_____
thanatophobia (death)	_____
tocophobia (childbirth)	_____
triskaidekaphobia (number 13)	_____
xenophobia (strangers)	_____
zoophobia (animals)	_____

. . . to list just a few. Then there are the manias, the obsessions. For instance, EGOMANIA (desiring to impress others; doing things like inventing big words to make yourself look intelligent, like some of the words in the list above!).

175

Let's make this simple. Heights, snakes, spiders, public speaking, etc., are all triggers of one extremely common emotion — FEAR!

If you didn't relate to the phobias listed on the previous page, how about the following *fears of*:

Abandonment
Accidents
Change   _____
Confrontation   _____
Criticism   _____
Dealing with issues   _____
Enemies   _____
Finances   _____
Fear itself
Flying   _____
Friends   _____
Having children
Life will change
Losing your job   _____
Loss of relationship   _____
Public speaking   _____
Rejection
Responsibility
Ridicule (what will people say?) _____
Sex   _____
The Unknown
The Future
Too much money
Your mother
  (or your father)   _____

(Fill in your own)

_____	_____
_____	_____
_____	_____
_____	_____

If you observe people, you'll recognize that they can be separated into two distinct categories: (1) people who feel the fear and take action anyway; and (2) people who let fear limit them. The only difference between these two categories is *a state of mind*.

If we don't recognize and admit fear in our lives, it can become a self-limiting force. Fear can limit us socially and romantically, for instance.

On the first day of school, most people look around the room to see who else is in the class. Once a young man noticed a very attractive blonde girl sitting in the back of the room. The next day, he was very disappointed when she didn't show up for the class. On the third day, he walked to the front of the room when he suddenly realized this charming young lady was sitting there with an empty seat beside her. He immediately felt shy and nervous, thinking he should take a seat at the back of the room. Feelings like these are fairly common to most people, who suffer from self-doubt or fear of rejection. "Would you like to sit down?" the young lady asked him.

"Why, yes, I would!" he replied.

Imagine you're at a party. You introduce two of your friends to each other. Both of them are intelligent, attractive people. You're aware that these people are immediately attracted to each other and that makes you feel good.

You felt that they would make an excellent couple, and it looks like you were right. You were already aware that the two of them had a lot in common and you're pleased that they seem to be "hitting it off." In order for this bond to be extended from a meeting at a party into a lasting relationship, one of the parties must take the initiative and overcome his or her fear of rejection enough to at least ask for a phone number or a date in the future.

This is the point at which lifelong friendships and romances hang in the balance. When people believe in themselves and act with self-confidence, they create relationships easily. For many, however, fear of rejection prevents them from finding love and fulfillment in their lives and they face loneliness and isolation. Friendships occur when people are willing to get out there and risk rejection. Actions become habits. Habits can be either positive or negative.

The encouraging thing is to realize that habits can be changed, once people recognize and identify their fears. Moving through fear and insecurity and risking rejection instead of accepting limitation allow an individual to create whatever quality of life he or she desires. When people feel fear and take action anyway, they've already paid the price to create the results they desire.

To say "I have no fear" is simply denial. That's the same as saying "I have no emotion, no excitement in my life." Fear originates in mental programming and that programming can be changed. Self-limitation due to fear is reversible.

Steven Bisyak & Michael McDermott

Wherever you go, whatever you do,
you can never run away from you. . . .
because wherever you go, there you are

Michael McDermott

When you face fear squarely, it disappears. It's like an illusion, appearing to be real, but when it's confronted, it vanishes. Fear is our emotional response to the experiences of life. It's a habitual response.

For instance, a baby has no innate fear of spiders. One day, the baby discovers a large spider and curiously starts playing with it. At that moment, the mother walks into the room, sees the spider, and begins screaming hysterically. Because the mother is screaming and upset, the baby is fearful. The baby automatically associates the mother's fear with the spider. So now we have the mother terrified and the baby petrified, to say nothing of the spider, which is probably scared out of its tiny mind. The spider didn't initially cause the fear, but the memory of the experience has been imprinted into the memory of the baby through the reticular activating system in the brain. Years later, the child who now has become an adult is fearful of spiders because of that scary experience, which has long ago been forgotten. Regardless of the fact that the original experience has been forgotten, the fear reaction is there.

The fear response has become ingrained in the individual.

Human beings are pleasure-seeking organisms. Pain is resisted at all costs and pleasure is pursued. Fear is avoided because it doesn't feel good. It's scary. It takes energy. By stepping through the fear, however, lives can be changed in positive ways.

Fear of the unknown is one of the fears most common to all human beings. Haunted houses are scary because you never know what's going to pop up at you. So are IRS audits!

Addictions are another way to avoid dealing with fear. Alcohol, tobacco, food, drugs, even sex can give a temporary escape from the powerful emotion of fear. In reality, there's no permanent escape from fear. Alcohol or drugs are no permanent solution, only a temporary escape. When the person comes down, the fear is still there. Eventually, it has to be faced.

Self-limitation is shutting down to new experiences because of fear. People are born unlimited by fear. Psychology tells us that the only innate fears we have are the fear of falling and the fear of loud noises. Fear is created by conditioning and one's reactions to life experiences. Fear actually becomes a habit when those reactions are repeated again and again.

Change begins when one steps out of old habits and accepts the challenges life has to offer. Accepting challenges can create positive changes in a person's life. Fear is:

False Evidence Appearing Real

Fear is energy. It's the emotion of excitement. It teaches us to pay attention to any given situation. It's not something to run from. *Love truly is letting go of fear.*

Faith can be defined as a positive belief. Faith is focusing on the best that could possibly happen. Whether it's called positive thinking, belief, trust, assurance, or conviction, this principle allows a person to take action regardless of the fear.

What is the state of mind that allows some people to be "fearless"? A person who acts fearlessly is one who has learned to feel the fear and take action anyway. Fear and love are two opposite states of mind. All negative action in life is based in fear. All positive action in life is based in love. There's no fear in love. Love casts out fear and other negative emotions such as jealousy, doubt, envy, and suspicion. Sometimes people sacrifice their lives helping others. In order to do that, fear must be confronted and accepted. For example, a comedian has to face the fear of rejection, or the fear that he might not be funny.

Positive action creates positive results. Mother Teresa is one example of love through remarkable service. People sometimes do dramatic things, such as jumping into a river and risking their lives to rescue someone. Firemen often rescue children and elderly people from burning buildings and sometimes they lose their own lives in the process. It is possible to overcome fear and take positive action. Heroes are made, not born. Sacrificing your life can also mean giving your time, because your time is your life.

Before people attempt an activity such as walking on fire, they often think about the worst that could possibly happen in the situation. Then they're instructed to let their horror thoughts go and just focus on the best that could possibly happen.

Worry arises in the mind when the entire focus is on worst-case scenarios. Imagination creates all kinds of pictures in the mind, positive and negative. Fear is caused by negative imagination. It's created by the power of the mind. It's much easier to face negative projections and negative imaginations than to live with fear forever.

Another reason fear arises is because of the value judgments that are placed on life experiences. Pain by ordinary standards is "bad" and pleasure is defined as "good." In reality, without pain or challenges there would be little, if any, real personal growth. Some of the "worst" things that ever happen to a person end up producing the most good. So things are not always what they appear to be, and there are silver linings to the clouds. It all depends on the perspective of the individual. Some people can focus on the best and "turn lemons into lemonade," while others turn wine into sour grapes. If life experiences are judged from a long-term perspective, it's easy to see that something that looks "bad" at first glance is not necessarily bad. Good and bad are different sides of the same coin. The "coin" is life experience. Experiences are neither good nor bad, they're just experiences. It's only value judgments that define experience as good or bad.

Carried to an extreme, fear causes greed. Fear causes separation and dissention. Fear causes war. A major reason people kill themselves is they don't know how to handle fear in their lives. Winston Churchill said, "We have nothing to fear but fear itself." On the contrary, it's not necessary to be afraid of fear if you know how to use fear as a positive energy in your life. If the emotion of fear is the same as that of excitement, there's nothing to fear about fear. If you realize that fear is excitement, fear can become something you actually look forward to.

Mastering fear brings serenity and peace of mind. No one can do it for you; you have to learn how to handle fear yourself. That's why in this book it's called The Ultimate Challenge. It's an inside job. You can't change anyone except yourself, and even that with great difficulty sometimes. Change has to start with one's self. Fear creates illusion. Separating the illusion of fear from the reality of experience, you can begin to create some very significant positive changes in your life.

There's little difference between the warrior and the coward. Both feel the same fear. The coward feels fear and runs. The warrior feels the same fear and fights.

Accept fear. Be honest about it. It's a common emotion in the human experience. It's not an enemy. In reality, fear is a familiar friend that comes around and taps you on the shoulder and says, "Hey! PAY ATTENTION to what you're doing." Taking action in spite of fear helps people develop courage, strength, and self-confidence.

Fear has a proper place in the realm of human experience. It's a reminder to *PAY ATTENTION* as you *GO FOR IT!!* There's no way to accept an exciting challenge without feeling some fear. Fear energy can help us live life to the fullest, if we use the energy of fear in a positive way.

21

CONCLUSION

Take the lessons you learn at the firewalk into your day-to-day life. Don't say, "Well, it works here at the firewalk, but it won't work out there in the real world." Just go out there and do it! Drop the old baggage. Free yourself of the negative programs you've been holding on to in your own mind. You will begin to see positive changes in your life.

Love yourself unconditionally. Love yourself with all your faults, all your fears, all your inadequacies. If you never get beyond that in this life, that's enough. If you love yourself, you'll be capable of loving others.

Last, here's a word to the skeptics out there among you. If you've read this far, there's probably a small opening somewhere in your mind. Allow for the possibilities that are suggested by the material we've presented here. Then go out and get some personal experience. Hope to see you all at a firewalk!

Focus on the best
Forget the rest!

Michael McDermott

Don't Horse Around. . .
JUST DO IT!!!

Mr. Ed

BLISS OR BLISTERS:
A Firewalker's Dictionary

AAAAAHHHHHHHHHAAHHHHAHHHHHHHHHHH!!!
Definition of a scream. Can happen when you bungee jump or skydive, or when you're having great sex. Screaming happens when fear turns into terror. You lose control. It's more or less automatic.

BLISTERED When you develop the ability to walk on water. The water collects in the bottom of your foot, sometimes the blister pops, and you leave water stains on the floor. You're literally "walking on water."

BODY PIERCING Looks like a really stupid thing to do. In reality it's an intense exercise in mind control, mastering pain and focusing body ki or the energies. A 100% focused mind can eliminate pain and bleeding. Body piercing is commonly done with a five-inch doll needle stuck through the hand between the thumb and index finger.

BULL!!! What you scream when you don't want fear to limit you. You scream as loudly as you can, and then you shuffle across the fire. Sometimes you scream the same thing when fear kicks in and you don't want to follow through. What you're really saying is, "I'm afraid. I want my mama. Get me out of here!!!!"

BURN Something that might put you in Bellevue or Harborview burn ward, depending on the degree of the burn and your ability to deal with your pain. For most minor burns it could be as simple as the application of hydrogen peroxide three times daily.

CLING-ON The bad guys on Star Trek. A hot coal that sticks to your foot after you're off the fire. Shake, shake, shake your foot. Shake it or bake it.

COOK You cook yourself because you're not paying attention or your mind is in to ego, doubt, or fear. The bottom of your foot might come off. You might crawl to the bathroom for a month. Cooking teaches you valuable lessons. The pain is so great, if you don't have ice to put on it, you might consider putting yourself out of your misery.

COURT REPORTER The part of the mind that screams things like, "You stupid fool! You're going to kill yourself! You idiot! You're going to die!! Don't do this! You don't have any insurance! You're going to end up in a wheelchair!"

EGO Fear and self-doubt causing you to focus on what others think of you. Desire to impress others is also ego. Ego will get you burned in the fire. Ego can also burn you in life.

ENDORPHINS Your body's own drug lab. These little bitty guys bliss you out so good that you don't even care what happens to you.

EXCITEMENT A signal that your energy's high. The body's energy response to what's going on in the mind.

FEAR *False Evidence Appearing Real.* Fear is the expectation of negative experience. Fear is created through negative mental projections. Once you start to see fear for what it really is, you can deal with it. Fear can prevent you from taking a risk at all; it can limit you if you allow it to.

FIRE The TEACHER of all TEACHERS. The fire "knows what you're thinking." If your thoughts are 100% focused, you can walk on fire without getting burned. If the ego gets involved, *you might toast yourself.* Fire has been know to burn the ego.

FIREWALK What happens when you shut down your critical judgment (court reporter), believe in yourself 100%, and do the "impossible" feat of walking across red-hot coals.

FOCUSING A "laser beam" from the mind. Concentrated mental energy during which you pay 100% attention.

FRY A milder way of saying you cooked yourself. You still might be able to walk, but don't count on it.

GNARLY Definition of a fire that makes you wish you were on that bus home! Most fires look gnarly when they are started. The flames shoot 15 feet high, way up into the air, and you ask yourself, "What the hell am I doing here?"

GO FOR IT In other words, take action. When you are in the moment, do it!

HARDCORES People who firewalk on a regular basis. They might run to the window in the morning and scan the horizon for smoke! They have a "burning desire" to master all fears.

HORROR THOUGHTS Your worst fears. The most frightening thing you can possibly imagine.

INNER GUIDANCE Still, small voice within; automatic body response. A connection with source energy. Something that most people need to learn to listen to. Intuition. Pay attention to it!

IN THE MOMENT Tiny, narrow window of opportunity. NOW. The time to take action. The window of opportunity that comes to all people. The moment of truth, when you either take action or you take the bus home.

LOG IN (to the mind) Deciding in advance what you'll do when a certain set of circumstances happens to you. If you log something in, you mentally program it to your future reality. You mentally rehearse; you visualize. When you do that, you'll automatically respond with the appropriate action when the circumstances occur in your life. Log in is mental programming of how you want to react in the moment.

MENTAL STATE State of mind that either limits you or allows you to do the "impossible."

OWWWEEEEEE Being out of focus when you get a cling-on.

PAY ATTENTION Your insurance policy against getting burned in the fire, in a relationship, or in your life.

PAYBACKS Basic Newtonian Physics, also called the law of KARMA. For every action, there is an equal and opposite reaction. You inevitably reap what you sow. If you burn someone in this life, they'll burn you in the next life. Conversely, the good you've done will come back to you. Paybacks are "a bitch."

PULLEY SWING A long cable with a rope attached to a pulley. You swing through the trees like Tarzan (or Jane). Pay attention to avoid killing yourself.

PYROMETER Scientific device for measuring the actual temperature of the fire.

RETICULAR ACTIVATING SYSTEM (R.A.S.) The part of the mind that recalls your past when you face a similar activity in the present. Causes an emotional reaction—for instance, when you see a spider or a snake.

SCARY Our perception of a person, place, or thing. Generally, we avoid scary things. Fear is a natural reaction to something we perceive as scary. A cat's back arches when the cat is fearful.

TERROR What you experience when fear gets so intense you totally lose it. Take a second pair of pants and extra briefs.

TRY The TERRIBLE "T" WORD. Try! It Sucks, Sucks, SUCKS!!!! Trying never did anything! Eliminate the word "try" from your vocabulary and replace it with "Do." *Take action and JUST DO IT!*

WAAAAAWHOOOOOOOOOOOOO!!!! A scream of fear mixed with ecstasy. A milder form of this would be when you scream WWWHHHEEEEEEEEE!!!!!!

ZINGER Could be the result of a cling-on, less intense than an OUWEE. Discomfort experienced when you feel heat. You got a "zinger."

Steven Bisyak & Michael McDermott are available for speaking engagements and firewalking trainings:

Challenges Unlimited, Inc./
Cords Unlimited, Inc.
PO Box 911
Snoqualmie, WA 98065
(206) 233-8060 (voicemail)

or:

Frog & Latté Publishing
P.O. Box 3073
Kirkland, WA 98083-3073
(206) 821-9050 (direct line)

CHALLENGES UNLIMITED TRAINING ("CUT")

CUT 1-4	Firewalking seminars; basic trainings
CUT 7	7-day Firewalk Teacher Certification ("FTC")
The Ultimate	2-3 weeks extended trainings

ONLY A PERSON WHO RISKS IS FREE

Latté Publishing
P.O. Box 3073
Kirkland, WA 98083-3073
(206) 821-9050

Please send _____ copies of "MASTERING FEAR:
The Ultimate Challenge"

I enclose $14.95 plus $2.00 ea. postage (Washington residents add sales tax)

Name_____

Address_____

City/State/Zip_____

Frog Publishing
P.O. Box 3073
Kirkland, WA 98083-3073
(206) 821-9050

Please send _____ copies of "STORIES OF THE
FIRE"

I enclose $14.95 plus $2.00 ea. postage (Washington residents add sales tax)

Name_____

Address_____

City/State/Zip_____